Quick-Guides to Inclusion 3

Quick-Guides to Inclusion 3

Ideas for Educating
Students with Disabilities

edited by

Michael F. Giangreco, Ph.D.
University of Vermont
Burlington

with contributions by

Karen A. Erickson, Ph.D.
Douglas Fisher, Ph.D.
Timothy Fox, M.Ed.
Cheryl M. Jorgensen, Ph.D.
David A. Koppenhaver, Ph.D.
Robi M. Kronberg, Ph.D.
Deborah Lisi-Baker
Irene McEwen, PT, Ph.D.
Zach Rossetti, M.Ed.
Carol Tashie, M.Ed.

and

Michael L. Wehmeyer, Ph.D.

·P A U L·H·
BROOKES
PUBLISHING C? ®

Baltimore • London • Toronto • Sydney

Paul H. Brookes Publishing Co.
Post Office Box 10624
Baltimore, Maryland 21285-0624

www.brookespublishing.com

Typeset by Integrated Publishing Solutions, Grand Rapids, Michigan.
Manufactured in the United States of America by
Versa Press, East Peoria, Illinois.

All royalties from the sale of this book are donated to nonprofit groups
or agencies that meet human needs.

The individuals and situations described in this book are completely
fictional or are based on composites of various people and circumstances,
in which case, pseudonyms have been used. Any similarity to actual individuals
or circumstances is coincidental, and no implications should be inferred.

Gender specifications alternate throughout the text.

Library of Congress Cataloging-in-Publication Data

Quick-guides to inclusion 3: ideas for educating students with disabilities / edited by Michael F.
   Giangreco; with contributions by Karen A. Erickson...[et al.].
      p.   cm.
   Includes bibliographical references.
   ISBN 1-55766-582-6
   1. Inclusive education.   2. Children with disabilities—Education.   I. Title: Quick-guides to inclu-
   sion three.   II. Giangreco, Michael F., 1956–   III. Erickson, Karen A.
LC1200 .Q85 2002
371.95'2—dc21   2002-018263

British Library Cataloguing in Publication are available from the British Library.

Contents

About the Editor vii

Contributors ix

What Are Quick-Guides and How Are They Used? xi

**Quick-Guide #11: Reaching and Teaching Diverse Learners Through
Differentiated Instruction**
Robi M. Kronberg 1

   1. Know Your Students 6
   2. Develop a Classroom Community Respectful of Diversity 8
   3. Create a "Working-With" Learning Environment 10
   4. Clarify Your Instructional Focus 12
   5. Ensure that All Students Have Access to the Curriculum 14
   6. Expand Your Instructional Repertoire 16
   7. Design Ways for Students to Demonstrate What They Know 18
   8. Assess Throughout Your Instruction 20
   9. Teach Students How to Be Effective Learners 22
  10. Develop a Workable System of Organization and Management 24

Quick-Guide #12: Supporting Literacy Learning in All Children
David A. Koppenhaver and Karen A. Erickson 29

   1. Focus Literacy Activities on Communication 34
   2. Use Word-Based Lessons 36
   3. Balance Your Instruction 38
   4. Make Materials Accessible for Every Student 40
   5. Provide Diverse Materials and Models 42
   6. Assess Word Identification, Reading Comprehension, and
      Listening Comprehension 44
   7. Teach Three-Part Reading Comprehension Lessons 46
   8. Use a Word Wall 48
   9. Teach the Writing Process 50
  10. Perfect Practice Makes Perfect 52

Quick-Guide #13:   Supporting Friendships For All Students
Carol Tashie and Zach Rossetti 57

  1.   Everyone Can and Should Have Friends 62
  2.   Model the Highest Expectations for All Students 64
  3.   Make Sure All Students Share Time, Space, and Activities 66
  4.   Not Being Able to Speak Is Not the Same as Having Nothing to Say 68
  5.   Create a Class that Truly Celebrates, Not Simply Tolerates, Diversity . 70
  6.   Don't Get in the Way—Respect the Space that Friendships Require 72
  7.   Recognize the Single Most Underutilized Resource in Schools:
       Students 74
  8.   You Can't Do it Alone—Families Are Essential 76
  9.   Pay Attention to What Friendship Is and Isn't 78
 10.   Provide Intentional Facilitation 80

Quick-Guide #14:   Self-Determination
Michael L. Wehmeyer 85

  1.   It Starts with Your Example: Model Problem Solving 90
  2.   Tell Students You Believe They Are Capable 92
  3.   Emphasize Student Strengths and Uniqueness 94
  4.   Create a Learning Community that Promotes Risk Taking 96
  5.   Structure Your Classroom to Promote Choice Making 98
  6.   Empower Students to Make Decisions and Set Goals 100
  7.   Teach Students Self-Determination Skills 102
  8.   Encourage Student-Directed Learning 104
  9.   Use Peers to Provide Supports 106
 10.   Advocate for Your Own Self-Determination 108

Quick-Guide #15:   Taking Inclusion to the Next Level:
Creating Inclusive High School Classrooms
Cheryl M. Jorgensen, Douglas Fisher, and Carol Tashie 113

  1.   Teach All High School Students Life's Most Important Lessons 118
  2.   Teach Students to Care About Learning by Caring About Them 120
  3.   Figure Out How Every Student Is "Smart" 122
  4.   Make Learning Relevant Through the Study of "Essential Questions" ... 124
  5.   Make Learning Cooperative 126
  6.   Allow Students a Variety of Ways to "Show What They Know" 128
  7.   When Students Need Intensive Supports, Provide Them as Naturally as
       Possible 130
  8.   Embed Social Justice Values in the Curriculum and Your Classroom ... 132
  9.   Become a Reflective Practitioner with Other Teachers in Your School . 134
 10.   Advocate for Untracking and the Inclusion of All Students 136

Quick-Guide Extra: Assisting Students Who Use Wheelchairs:
Guidelines for School Personnel
Michael F. Giangreco, Irene McEwen, Timothy Fox, and Deborah Lisi-Baker 141

About the Editor

Michael F. Giangreco, Ph.D., Research Associate Professor, Center on Disability and Community Inclusion, University of Vermont, 101 Cherry Street, Suite 450, Burlington, Vermont 05401

Michael F. Giangreco has spent more than 25 years working with children and adults in a variety of capacities including special education teacher, community residence counselor, camp counselor, school administrator, educational consultant, university teacher, and researcher. Dr. Giangreco received a bachelor's degree from the State University of New York—College at Buffalo and graduate degrees from the University of Vermont and the University of Virginia. He received his doctoral degree from Syracuse University and has been a faculty member at the University of Vermont since 1988.

His work and educational experiences have led Dr. Giangreco to focus his research, training, and other work activities on three interrelated aspects of educating students with and without disabilities in their local general education schools: 1) individualized curriculum planning, 2) adapting curriculum and instruction, and 3) coordinating support services in schools. Dr. Giangreco is the author of numerous professional publications, including **Choosing Outcomes and Accommodations for Children (COACH): A Guide to Educational Planning for Students with Disabilities, Second Edition,** with Chigee J. Cloninger and Virginia Salce Iverson (Paul H. Brookes Publishing Co., 1998); the first two sets of **Quick-Guides to Inclusion: Ideas for Educating Students with Disabilities** (Paul H. Brookes Publishing Co., 1997, 1998); and **Vermont Interdependent Services Team Approach (VISTA): A Guide to Coordinating Educational Support Services** (Paul H. Brookes Publishing Co., 1996).

Beginning in 1998, he collaborated with artist Kevin Ruelle to complete an unusual project consisting of three sets of educational cartoons:

1. *Ants in His Pants* (Peytral Publications, 1998)
2. *Flying by the Seat of His Pants* (Peytral Publications, 1999)
3. *Teaching Old Logs New Tricks* (Peytral Publications, 2000)

Dr. Giangreco's work has been advanced by the feedback and input of innumerable students (with or without disabilities), parents, teachers, administrators, related services providers, and other colleagues.

Contributors

Karen A. Erickson, Ph.D.
Associate Research Professor
Center for Literacy and Disability
    Studies
CB# 7335
University of North Carolina at
    Chapel Hill
Chapel Hill, North Carolina 27599

Douglas Fisher, Ph.D.
Director of Professional Development
School of Education
San Diego State University
5850 Hardy Avenue, Suite 112
San Diego, California 92182

Timothy Fox, M.Ed.
Center on Disability and Community
    Inclusion
University of Vermont
101 Cherry Street, Suite 450
Burlington, Vermont 05401

Cheryl M. Jorgensen, Ph.D.
Project Coordinator
Institute on Disability
University of New Hampshire
7 Leavitt Lane
Durham, New Hampshire 03824

David A. Koppenhaver, Ph.D.
Pehrson Chair in Education
Gustavus Adolphus College
800 West College Street
St. Peter, Minnesota 56082

Robi M. Kronberg, Ph.D.
Educational Consultant
4573 East Lake Circle North
Littleton, Colorado 80121

Deborah Lisi-Baker
Executive Director
Vermont Center for Independent
    Living
11 East State Street
Montpelier, Vermont 05602

Irene McEwen, PT, Ph.D.
Presidential Professor
Presbyterian Health Foundation
University of Oklahoma Health
    Sciences Center
Division of Rehabilitation
Post Office Box 26901
801 N.E. 13th Street
Oklahoma City, Oklahoma 73190

Zach Rossetti, M.Ed.
Inclusion Facilitator
Memorial Drive School
10 Memorial Drive
Farmington, New Hampshire 03835

Carol Tashie, M.Ed.
Project Coordinator
Institute on Disability
University of New Hampshire
10 Ferry Street, #14
Concord, New Hampshire 03301

Michael L. Wehmeyer, Ph.D.
Research Associate Professor
Beach Center on Disability
University of Kansas
Haworth Hall, Room 3136
Lawrence, Kansas 66045

What Are Quick-Guides and How Are They Used?

Many educators whom we meet are anxious to get relevant information on inclusive education but find that they don't have enough time to read long articles and books. We have designed the Quick-Guides contained in this book (#11 through #15) to provide helpful advice that can be read in a short amount of time. Guides #11 through #15 expand on information provided in Guides #1 through #5 (*Quick Guides to Inclusion: Ideas for Educating Students with Disabilities* [Paul H. Brookes Publishing Co., 1997]) and Guides #6 through #10 (*Quick Guides to Inclusion 2: Ideas for Educating Students with Disabilities* [Paul H. Brookes Publishing Co., 1998]).

You may consider each of the Quick-Guides in this book as an individual document that can stand alone, even though the Quick-Guides are interrelated.

Each Quick-Guide has

- A letter to the teacher that introduces the content
- A list of 10 Guidelines-at-a-Glance
- A set of the guidelines, each on a separate page, suitable for duplication as overhead transparencies
- A page of text discussing each of the 10 guidelines
- A short list of selected references

The Quick-Guides are written for general education teachers, although they can be helpful to a variety of team members. You have permission to photocopy the Quick-Guides from this book to share with your colleagues (please see the photocopying guidelines on page iv). We thought this might be especially helpful for those of you who find yourself working with other general education teachers to facilitate the supported education of students with disabilities. As we shared these Quick-Guides prior to publication, we found they were frequently given to general educators by special education colleagues, were passed out to faculty members by their principal, and were used by staff development specialists and trainers as part of information packets. Some people used them to share information with parents, paraeducators, therapists, community members, school board members, student teachers, and college students.

We have made all of the **Quick-Guides 3** content available as an e-book on-line at **www.brookespublishing.com/qg3.** You can visit this site to reference Quick-Guides #11–#15 (and the Quick-Guides Extra) or to download a specific guide. We hope this will aid your collaboration efforts and provide you with a quick and easy way to share this information.

We encourage you to share the guides with folks—that's the whole idea! If you have any ideas about future Quick-Guide topics, please feel free to contact me.

Good luck!

Michael F. Giangreco

Quick-Guides to Inclusion 3

Quick-Guide #11

Reaching and Teaching Diverse Learners Through Differentiated Instruction

Robi M. Kronberg

Quick-Guides to Inclusion 3: Ideas for Educating Students with Disabilities

Michael F. Giangreco
Series Editor

Dear Teacher,

Your classroom is probably more diverse than it ever has been. Your students have a myriad of learning characteristics and interests. You have some students who struggle with reading, whereas others seem to be able to read everything. You might also have students who speak a primary language other than English. Some of your students love attending school, and others find little relevance in what school has to offer. Your task of teaching this diverse set of students is a daunting one—especially with the additional pressure many teachers feel surrounding testing and standards.

Before you succumb to feeling totally overwhelmed … stop and reflect. You already know how to teach students with differing characteristics and needs—that's what differentiation is all about. Your skills at differentiating instruction may not be at the level that you would like, but you do have a starting point from which to build. You have the capacity to reach and teach all of your diverse students.

The following guidelines are designed to provide you with ideas about important aspects of differentiation. Take differentiation one step at a time. Start at a place that feels comfortable—try a few new ideas and build on your successes. Share your ideas, as well as your frustrations, with your colleagues. Strengthening the skillfulness of your teaching has never been so challenging or so important.

Sincerely,

Robi

GUIDELINES-AT-A-GLANCE

1. Know Your Students

2. Develop a Classroom Community Respectful of Diversity

3. Create a "Working-With" Learning Environment

4. Clarify Your Instructional Focus

5. Ensure that All Students Have Access to the Curriculum

6. Expand Your Instructional Repertoire

7. Design Ways for Students to Demonstrate What They Know

8. Assess Throughout Your Instruction

9. Teach Students How to Be Effective Learners

10. Develop a Workable System of Organization and Management

Quick-Guides to Inclusion 3: Ideas for Educating Students with Disabilities © Michael F. Giangreco 2002
Available through Paul H. Brookes Publishing Co., Baltimore: 1-800-638-3775

#1.

Know Your Students

Know Your Students

The most important aspect of your diverse classroom is your students. Your ability to effectively reach and teach your students depends on knowing them—knowing their interests, learning styles, strengths, needs, and skills. There are many possibilities for getting to know your students. Student interests can be discovered by providing interest inventories, having students interview each other, facilitating a class discussion, observing your students, and having conversations with them. Differentiation will be enhanced as you guide students to particular reading selections, encourage them to pursue in-depth investigations in an area of interest, or design activities that invite students to learn in ways that are engaging and meaningful.

Your students reflect a mosaic of life experiences and learning characteristics. Students' prior knowledge and experiences can be determined through teacher inquiry—"How many of you have ever been to a museum?" "Who can describe a mammal?" "Why are some governments democracies?" Selecting learning outcomes at the correct level of difficulty can be determined through pre-assessment or teacher knowledge of student performance. Understanding what your students bring to each learning experience will inform you as to how best to design instruction at each students' level of challenge.

Your students will also have different learning styles. Some students will learn best by listening, some by watching, and others by doing. Knowing the learning styles of your students will assist you in designing a balance of instructional opportunities.

Quick-Guides to Inclusion 3: Ideas for Educating Students with Disabilities © Michael F. Giangreco 2002
Available through Paul H. Brookes Publishing Co., Baltimore: 1–800–638–3775

#2

Develop a Classroom Community Respectful of Diversity

Develop a Classroom Community Respectful of Diversity

Establishing a sense of community is an essential ingredient for creating a successful differentiated classroom. All students want to contribute, be respected, and be cared about. Your classroom will provide fertile ground for helping students learn how to value differences; appreciate commonalities; and come to deeper understandings of such complex issues as fairness, cooperation, equity, and justice. Teachers concur that building a classroom community takes time and intentionality. Students need support in understanding why differentiated instruction is important.

Proactively establishing classroom expectations is important. For example, a fifth-grade teacher establishes expectations in the context of teaching about the preamble of the U.S. Constitution by having students create their own preamble—one that will guide their behavior throughout the year—after learning about the purpose. Many teachers find that class meetings are helpful vehicles for addressing issues, mediating conflict, and planning instructional activities—in general, working together as a community of learners.

Identifying student strengths and highlighting the array of strengths present among students is also important. A high school teacher provides his students with information about learning styles and multiple intelligences as a way of increasing self-awareness. All students use their learning profile to guide choice-making and to enhance reflection.

The time taken to create a classroom community is time well spent. Mutual respect and understanding form a strong foundation on which to build a differentiated classroom.

Quick-Guides to Inclusion 3: Ideas for Educating Students with Disabilities © Michael F. Giangreco 2002
Available through Paul H. Brookes Publishing Co., Baltimore: 1-800-638-3775

#3

Create a "Working-With" Learning Environment

Quick-Guides to Inclusion 3: Ideas for Educating Students with Disabilities © Michael F. Giangreco 2002
Available through Paul H. Brookes Publishing Co., Baltimore: 1-800-638-3775

Create a "Working-With" Learning Environment

Differentiated classrooms are learning environments where teachers and students work together to create relevant and meaningful learning opportunities. Creating a "working-with" classroom environment means that teachers and students share decisions about instructional activities, ways in which students might work together, and how students can demonstrate their learning. Teachers who create working-with learning environments encourage students to build responsibility in monitoring their work habits, make choices to enhance their learning, self-assess quality of work, and help make decisions about how the overall classroom is functioning.

For example, during a fifth-grade class meeting, a teacher asks her students to discuss how different tasks might be assigned in order to complete a cooperative group project. An eighth-grade teacher frames the targeted learning outcomes for an upcoming unit and asks his students to work in small groups to brainstorm instructional activities that would assist the students in reaching their benchmarks. A high school science teacher asks her students to select three lab partners that will create a group comprised of students with complementary learning strengths.

Working-with environments are sometimes messy and unpredictable. When you ask for student input, you don't always know what to expect! The benefits, however, are far reaching. Students acquire lifelong skills of self-directedness, share responsibility for their learning, learn to appreciate the value of different opinions, and benefit from the ideas of their classmates. A working-with environment creates a classroom community where everyone is a teacher and a learner.

Quick-Guides to Inclusion 3: Ideas for Educating Students with Disabilities © Michael F. Giangreco 2002
Available through Paul H. Brookes Publishing Co., Baltimore: 1-800-638-3775

#4

Clarify Your Instructional Focus

Clarify Your Instructional Focus

Thoughtful differentiation requires clarity of instruction. As you plan each unit of study, identify desired learning outcomes and establish clarity in three areas. First, determine what you want your students to *know*. In each unit, there are probably certain facts that you want your students to master. For example, it may be important for students to know that oxygen is a gas, to identify characteristics of insects, to list key events during the Civil War, or to define parts of speech.

Second, be clear as to what you want your students to *understand*. Each unit should engage the students in understanding relevant concepts and principles. For example, it may be important that students understand the concept of measurement and an accompanying principle that there are different methods and systems of measurement.

Third, be specific in what you want students to *be able to do* as a result of their engagement with the curriculum. The skills that you target for your students may involve summarizing information, utilizing a graphic organizer, interpreting data, solving an equation, or giving an oral presentation.

Clarity of your instructional focus is at the heart of differentiation. Opportunities are created when factual, conceptual, and skill-based areas are combined. Once you have established clarity, you will make many decisions about how to support students in learning. You must also decide how each student can best understand the concepts and principles—some students will need concrete experiences, whereas others will be ready for abstract applications. Achieving student mastery of the identified skills will also require thoughtful differentiation.

Quick-Guides to Inclusion 3: Ideas for Educating Students with Disabilities © Michael F. Giangreco 2002
Available through Paul H. Brookes Publishing Co., Baltimore: 1-800-638-3775

#5

Ensure that All Students Have Access to the Curriculum

Ensure that All Students Have Access to the Curriculum

Differentiated instruction is an inclusive way of teaching and learning. Ideally, planning for differentiation occurs within a collaborative framework. Hopefully, the collaborators include both general as well as special educators. When varied expertise areas are included, curricular planning becomes supportive of all students' learning needs. As proactively voiced by one middle school team, "We try not to modify the general education curriculum. As a team, we create curricular activities that are accessible to as many students as possible regardless of their challenges."

As teachers proactively plan how to ensure accessibility to the curricular content, they consider a variety of options for differentiation—both in the depth and breadth of content as well as how each student best acquires the content. For example, in a science unit on insects, a third-grade teacher encourages some of her students to explore how different insects adapt to environmental factors. Her plans for other students involve identifying familiar insects and investigating their characteristics. A few students will spend several days doing research in the library. In preparing for the unit, she has gathered a "tub" of resources that include grade-level reading material, resources rich with photographs and light on words, several audiotapes, a list of web sites, and several three-dimensional models of insects. In collaboration with a special education colleague, she has also included a teacher-made "unit dictionary" that captures essential vocabulary words and key concepts. By providing varied resources that capitalize on student interests and varying needs, this teacher supports all students in accessing the curriculum.

Quick-Guides to Inclusion 3: Ideas for Educating Students with Disabilities © Michael F. Giangreco 2002 Available through Paul H. Brookes Publishing Co., Baltimore: 1-800-638-3775

#6

Expand Your
Instructional
Repertoire

Expand Your Instructional Repertoire

Differentiation is all about creating multiple pathways for learning. Standards provide the targets for learning—differentiated instruction provides the various routes through which students attain mastery of identified learning outcomes. It is both the artistry and the skill of teaching that enable a teacher to continually expand his instructional repertoire in order to better meet the diverse needs of his students.

For example, a learning outcome in language arts involves knowing specific literary elements. A teacher strives for all of his students to reach mastery in understanding the element of setting. Based on his knowledge of his students, he creates options. One student, who struggles with English, uses a sequential graphic organizer to identify aspects of setting. Another student utilizes a software program that allows her to list descriptive terms and then create a web of categories. Two other students work together to create an alternative setting and then analyze how the new setting would alter the story. After all the students have had opportunities to understand setting, the teacher facilitates a large-group activity in which students share their understanding of the role of setting in literature.

In a differentiated classroom, it is accepted that students learn differently. What works for one student doesn't necessarily work for another. Don't forget to use your students as resources—they can share responsibility in suggesting various routes to a common destination. As one high school student remarked, "Words on a page don't talk to me. I need to be able to work in groups and talk about the stuff we need to learn."

Quick-Guides to Inclusion 3: Ideas for Educating Students with Disabilities © Michael F. Giangreco 2002
Available through Paul H. Brookes Publishing Co., Baltimore: 1-800-638-3775

#7

Design Ways
for Students
to Demonstrate
What They Know

Design Ways for Students to Demonstrate What They Know

In addition to creating multiple pathways for learning, differentiation also involves designing a variety of ways in which students can integrate and demonstrate what they have learned. Often thought of as products or projects, these culminating activities encourage students to synthesize what they have learned. Differences in students' interests, strengths, and needs will naturally lead to differences in how students demonstrate what they have learned.

An eighth-grade math teacher has developed three culminating activities for the unit on ratios, proportions, and percentages. Students select from the following: making a three-dimensional replica of an item that is 225% larger than the original item; designing an activity that would clarify the relationships between ratios, percentages, and proportions; or finding examples in one's life (captured by drawings, words, or photos) that depict relevant applications of ratios, percentages, and proportions. The teacher provides clear expectations as to what each product must include. She and the students have also agreed to use a rubric to assess the finished product.

As you plan for product differentiation, be mindful that students often require assistance with both the content focus of the project as well as the logistics of how best to successfully complete the project. Be prepared to offer support for the student who needs content clarification as well as the student who needs help with organizing materials or developing a checklist to keep track of project tasks and timelines.

Quick-Guides to Inclusion 3: Ideas for Educating Students with Disabilities © Michael F. Giangreco 2002 Available through Paul H. Brookes Publishing Co., Baltimore: 1–800–638–3775

#8

Assess Throughout Your Instruction

Assess Throughout Your Instruction

Assessment and differentiation are integrally linked. In differentiated classrooms, assessment occurs throughout instruction. It serves to inform both the teacher and the student of the current level of understanding, progress, effectiveness of teaching and learning, and areas in need of improvement or enrichment.

Formative assessment, done at the beginning of instruction, informs a teacher as to the range of "starting points" for each student. At the beginning of a science unit, a middle school teacher asks his students to write a best guess definition of the word *catalyst*. Based on their responses, the teacher designs differentiated activities that allow each student to work from his or her starting point. A second-grade teacher encourages students to brainstorm ideas about a particular concept and then creates a class web to help students begin to sort and label aspects of the concept.

Assessment can also be done throughout instruction. A sixth-grade teacher helps her students self-assess their progress on a 4-week project by creating a "benchmark timeline" of weekly tasks. At the end of each week, students initial the timeline indicating where they are in the task sequence. This visual provides a picture of progress as well as informing the teacher which students might be having difficulty with task pacing.

Summative assessment, done at the end of instruction, provides feedback as to how well students have mastered learning outcomes. In the spirit of differentiation, summative assessment should also allow for individual differences and strengths. Be creative, think inclusively, and ask students how they can best demonstrate what they have learned!

Quick-Guides to Inclusion 3: Ideas for Educating Students with Disabilities © Michael F. Giangreco 2002
Available through Paul H. Brookes Publishing Co., Baltimore: 1-800-638-3775

#9

Teach Students
How to Be
Effective Learners

Teach Students How to Be Effective Learners

Differentiated instruction changes the roles of students as well as teachers. In differentiated classrooms, students are active participants in the learning process. Student responsibilities include demonstrating such skills as making effective choices, being self-directed, organizing learning materials, and working cooperatively with classmates. Teachers must provide many guided opportunities for students to build competence and confidence in the skills needed to be productive and responsible learners.

Providing choices to students is a powerful motivator. Students need to learn how to make choices that will support their learning. A first-grader might choose between two learning center activities. A fifth-grader might be asked for input about a classroom seating arrangement. A seventh-grader might meet with his teacher to select a culminating project at an appropriate level of challenge.

Facilitating a successful differentiated classroom also will be enhanced by student skills of self-directedness. Elementary students might be taught to follow a learning contract in which tasks are specified, but the student selects the order in which the tasks are completed. Secondary students might develop a timeline to manage a multifaceted assignment. Cooperative skills also need to be taught and nurtured. A kindergarten student could work on sharing materials. A fourth-grade class might designate a student to complete a summary of the day's activities for an absent classmate. High school students might routinely edit each other's written work. Students need ongoing support to become effective learners. Seize those teachable moments, and offer lots of learning opportunities!

Quick-Guides to Inclusion 3: Ideas for Educating Students with Disabilities © Michael F. Giangreco 2002
Available through Paul H. Brookes Publishing Co., Baltimore: 1-800-638-3775

#10

Develop a Workable System of Organization and Management

Develop a Workable System of Organization and Management

Reaching and teaching all of your students can feel overwhelming. In addition to sharpening your instructional skills, collaborating with colleagues, and supporting students in taking an active role in their own learning, you will also want to develop some methods for organizing and managing your differentiated classroom. Here are some tips:

1. Have students practice "organizational logistics." Provide opportunities to practice the simple things (e.g., moving between learning centers, obtaining materials, utilizing co-operative role cards). This can help the instructional activity go more smoothly.

2. Develop set routines for giving directions. Multiple tasks, often requiring different directions, can be confusing. Establish routines that simplify directions. Color coding works well—teach students that if they are in the blue group or working on the blue set of tasks, then their materials are in the blue folder and the directions are written in blue on the overhead.

3. Give students responsibility for being accountable. You don't have to feel responsible for everything! If students in your class routinely turn in assignments, put them in charge of record keeping. Simply attach a list of student names to the outside of the assignment folder. As students turn in assignments, it is their responsibility to check off their name. You can, at a glance, see who has yet to turn in the assignment.

4. Utilize your students as resources. Designate class experts who can offer assistance to classmates in a myriad of ways. Implement an "Ask three before me rule" to encourage students to seek out classmates for help. Put your classroom community of teachers and learners to work!

Quick-Guides to Inclusion 3: Ideas for Educating Students with Disabilities © Michael F. Giangreco 2002
Available through Paul H. Brookes Publishing Co., Baltimore: 1-800-638-3775

Selected References

Cole, R. (Ed.). (1995). *Educating everybody's children: Diverse teaching strategies for diverse learners.* Alexandria, VA: Association for Supervision and Curriculum Development.

Cole, R. (Ed.). (2001). *More strategies for educating everybody's children.* Alexandria, VA: Association for Supervision and Curriculum Development.

Ellison, L. (1993). *Seeing with magic glasses.* Arlington, VA: Great Ocean Publishers.

Harmin, M. (1995). *Strategies to inspire active learning.* Edwardsville, IL: Inspiring Strategy Institute.

Marzano, R., Pickering, D., & Pollock, J. (2001). *Classroom instruction that works: Research-based strategies for increasing student achievement.* Alexandria, VA: Association for Supervision and Curriculum Development.

Silver, H., Strong, R., & Perini, M. (2000). *So each may learn: Integrating learning styles and multiple intelligences.* Alexandria, VA: Association for Supervision and Curriculum Development.

Tomlinson, C. (1999). *The differentiated classroom: Responding to the needs of all learners.* Alexandria, VA: Association for Supervision and Curriculum Development.

Tomlinson, C. (2001). *How to differentiate instruction in mixed-ability classrooms (2nd ed.).* Alexandria, VA: Association for Supervision and Curriculum Development.

Tomlinson, C., & Allan, S. (2000). *Leadership for differentiating schools & classrooms.* Alexandria, VA: Association for Supervision and Curriculum Development.

Quick-Guide #12

Supporting Literacy Learning in All Children

David A. Koppenhaver and Karen A. Erickson

Quick-Guides to Inclusion 3:
Ideas for Educating Students with Disabilities

Michael F. Giangreco
Series Editor

Quick-Guides to Inclusion 3: Ideas for Educating Students with Disabilities © Michael F. Giangreco 2002
Available through Paul H. Brookes Publishing Co., Baltimore: 1-800-638-3775

Dear Teacher,

Finding a way to teach all of the children in your class to read and write is a challenge, given the diversity of their experiences and abilities as well as the politically charged nature of literacy instruction. Just when you find a set of instructional strategies that work for you and meet the wide range of abilities of most of the children in your class, a new approach comes along, or a child with a particular set of special needs arrives, and you are challenged to throw out the old and bring in the new.

The 10 guidelines in this Quick-Guide are intended to provide some decision-making support as you face these challenges. Each guideline is followed by a brief explanation that will help you identify the strategies you already have in your arsenal and those areas in which new strategies might be needed. At the end of this Quick-Guide, you'll find selected references that will help you learn more about literacy instruction, assessment, and the use of assistive technologies to support all children in learning to read, write, and communicate.

This Quick-Guide is not filled with a new "right way" to teach. It is, instead, filled with some principles of successful classroom practice intended to help you find a balance that will benefit all of your students.

Read on!

David and Karen

GUIDELINES-AT-A-GLANCE

1. Focus Literacy Activities on Communication

2. Use Word-Based Lessons

3. Balance Your Instruction

4. Make Materials Accessible for Every Student

5. Provide Diverse Materials and Models

6. Assess Word Identification, Reading Comprehension, and Listening Comprehension

7. Teach Three-Part Reading Comprehension Lessons

8. Use a Word Wall

9. Teach the Writing Process

10. Perfect Practice Makes Perfect

Quick-Guides to Inclusion 3: Ideas for Educating Students with Disabilities © Michael F. Giangreco 2002
Available through Paul H. Brookes Publishing Co., Baltimore: 1-800-638-3775

#1

Focus Literacy Activities on Communication

Focus Literacy Activities on Communication

Communication is at the heart of learning to read and write. Without a focus on making and conveying meaning, literacy instruction can teach the skills but won't lead to lifelong use of those skills. In the early stages of learning to read and write, this means the focus should be on the functions of print rather than the form. In other words, students should be learning how and why their name is used in print rather than spending hours tracing their name or practicing the perfect formation of its letters. Students should be learning that storybook reading is about weaving a tale that is reflective of the pictures and the dozens of readings they have heard, rather than recognizing the handful of sight words they have memorized.

As students become more sophisticated in their reading and writing, this focus on communication means that students should select their own topics for writing and their own purposes for reading. Rather than always writing for reasons that others select, they should decide for themselves what they will write and who their audience will be. In the process, they'll learn powerful communication skills that are linked to content and contexts that they find meaningful. Within reading lessons, teachers should design reading comprehension tasks that require students to engage one another in meaningful conversations based on the texts they have read, rather than individually answering questions or completing assignments.

Regardless of a student's level of competence with reading or writing, linking literacy to communication increases the power of instruction and the likelihood that the skills will be used for a lifetime.

Quick-Guides to Inclusion 3: Ideas for Educating Students with Disabilities © Michael F. Giangreco 2002
Available through Paul H. Brookes Publishing Co., Baltimore: 1-800-638-3775

#2

Use Word-Based Lessons

Use Word-Based Lessons

We see it too often—children who have learned the rules of phonics can decode long lists of nonsense words and can demonstrate progress on standardized reading assessments but can't read or spell the words they encounter throughout their school day. Although phonics instruction is a valuable part of any balanced approach to teaching reading, in order for the abstract concepts to be useful in reading and writing, children must be taught using real words.

Asking students who are not yet proficient in reading and writing to learn a rule-based approach to reading and spelling is like asking someone to learn to play golf by reading the rulebook and occasionally going to a driving range. In the absence of time on a golf course and understanding the ultimate goal of getting the ball in the hole, learning to play golf is quite difficult. The same goes for phonics. Without real words and meaningful texts as the basis for phonics instruction, we are setting students up for a nearly impossible task. Certainly, students can learn the rules and apply them in the restricted context of word lists and phonics drills, but if they aren't able to use those skills in reading the books they want to read or writing the texts they want to write, what is the purpose?

A real-word approach to phonics teaches students to use words they know to figure out words they don't know. This approach is more likely to help students learn to read unfamiliar words like literate adults do by identifying familiar chunks rather than identifying individual phonemes (sounds) in the word from beginning to end and blending the sounds together.

Quick-Guides to Inclusion 3: Ideas for Educating Students with Disabilities © Michael F. Giangreco 2002
Available through Paul H. Brookes Publishing Co., Baltimore: 1-800-638-3775

#3

Balance Your Instruction

Balance Your Instruction

Children learn to read in different ways. Some learn from the rich interactions of being read storybooks by their parents or other family members. Some make significant strides once they have formally been taught the relationship between letters and sounds. Others make sense of print by exploring its forms and uses in their own writing attempts.

In classrooms with diverse groups of children, you must continually make adjustments to address the needs of all students. One successful way that teachers have done this is by providing a balance of instructional approaches and learning activities. Balance is different from the eclectic approach many of us have chosen over the years by taking a little of this, maybe a lot of that, some more of something else, and then settling on a mix that suits our teaching philosophy and expectations. Balance means that teachers make a conscious attempt to provide specific amounts of different instructional approaches.

In literacy instruction, the balance many teachers have found successful is to devote 30 minutes or more each day to four approaches: 1) guided reading, 2) composition, 3) word-level instruction, and 4) self-directed reading. In guided reading, you teach strategies for comprehending different kinds of texts. In composition, you create a writer's workshop in your classroom to support children in all components of the writing process. In word-level instruction, you help children learn phonics, sight words, and strategies for figuring out words they don't automatically recognize when reading. In self-directed reading, you create an environment where students share their interests in different kinds of reading and writing experiences to increase their motivation to read and write beyond the classroom.

Quick-Guides to Inclusion 3: Ideas for Educating Students with Disabilities © Michael F. Giangreco 2002
Available through Paul H. Brookes Publishing Co., Baltimore: 1-800-638-3775

#4

Make Materials Accessible for Every Student

Make Materials Accessible for Every Student

A book is not a book, nor a pencil a pencil, if a student isn't able to use it. We need to adapt or create tools for literacy learning that children with physical disabilities can hold, children with sensory impairments can see and hear, children with cognitive impairments can understand, and that all children are motivated to use.

As you consider the ways in which to create or adapt accessible tools, we suggest that you consider six dimensions of difference: communicative, cognitive, physical, sensory, affective, and attentional. These differences are significant because they affect the relative success or difficulty that children experience when using print-based materials. Children may have significant differences in one or more of the six dimensions and may, therefore, require multiple adaptations to existing materials in order to use them successfully.

Some of the most common means of adapting off-the-shelf materials can be accomplished with simple, everyday materials. For example, build up a pencil with some molding clay, make the pages of a book easier to turn by slipping them into plastic page protectors, or make a piece of paper easier to write on by taping it to the top of a 3-inch, three-ring binder with the fat side facing away from the student. Some high-tech methods of making print materials accessible include typing the text from a book into a talking word processor or screen reader, scanning a storybook and uploading it into a multimedia program that reads and allows page turning, or using an on-screen or alternative keyboard to support writing. Whatever solutions you find, don't allow the time it takes you to make the material accessible exceed the time the student will spend interacting with it!

Quick-Guides to Inclusion 3: Ideas for Educating Students with Disabilities © Michael F. Giangreco 2002
Available through Paul H. Brookes Publishing Co., Baltimore: 1-800-638-3775

#5

Provide Diverse Materials and Models

Provide Diverse Materials and Models

As teachers, we want to equip our students not only with the "hows" of reading but also with the "whys." We can do this by helping students make personal connections to literacy through both materials and strategies.

Find pencils and reading materials that children can *and want* to use. Entice students with cover art by standing some books upright on your shelves. Place books in strategic locations where students congregate, such as shelves in the bathroom, in the hall outside the lunchroom, or by the drinking fountain. Try to include at least 20 different kinds of reading materials per student in your class including newspapers, magazines, books (on CD), web sites, catalogs, cereal boxes, brochures, and atlases. Make sure that you have examples of fiction, nonfiction, directions, poetry, and plays. Include materials ranging from easy reading (even wordless picture books or comics) to narrative text.

Select strategies intended to create a classroom literacy community. Bring in a half dozen books, share a page or an idea that you think will attract student attention, and then make these books available to students. Read aloud to students, and structure the conversation around making personal connections. What would you have done in this character's place? What do you think might happen next? Set up a reader's chair and an author's chair for students to share what they're enjoying reading or writing. At the end of each day, ask yourself, "What did I do to encourage each of my students to choose to read or write when they don't have to?"

Quick-Guides to Inclusion 3: Ideas for Educating Students with Disabilities © Michael F. Giangreco 2002
Available through Paul H. Brookes Publishing Co., Baltimore: 1-800-638-3775

#6

Assess Word Identification, Reading Comprehension, and Listening Comprehension

---

Assess Word Identification, Reading Comprehension, and Listening Comprehension

When trying to understand why a student is having difficulty learning to read, base your search for understanding on the question, "Why can't this student read with comprehension at a higher grade level?" rather than, "Why doesn't this student read at grade level?" To answer the question, compare relative abilities in silent reading and listening comprehension, word identification, and phonics/decoding without regard to the child's age. The results will guide instructional decision making more effectively than a standardized test score.

Too often, norm-referenced standardized tests do not reveal the true source of a student's reading difficulty. For example, a 16-year-old was assessed yearly using a standard battery of norm-referenced tests. The tests suggested he read like a beginner in all areas, and the resulting instruction focused on phonemic awareness and phonics. Despite years of instruction, he was failing school and feared he would never pass the competency test his state required to graduate from high school. A comparison of his previously suggested abilities revealed that he could decode words through the sixth-grade level; however, he could read only a few words with automaticity and comprehend text through listening or silent reading at the second-grade level.

What did he need in order to read successfully at a higher grade level? He needed instruction focused on building fluency or automaticity in word reading, knowledge of the world, and comprehension strategies using materials that were both interesting and easy for him. He needed his educational team to look at his relative strengths and weaknesses as a reader as they planned his instructional program.

Quick-Guides to Inclusion 3: Ideas for Educating Students with Disabilities © Michael F. Giangreco 2002
Available through Paul H. Brookes Publishing Co., Baltimore: 1-800-638-3775

#7

Teach Three-Part Reading Comprehension Lessons

Quick-Guides to Inclusion 3: Ideas for Educating Students with Disabilities © Michael F. Giangreco 2002
Available through Paul H. Brookes Publishing Co., Baltimore: 1-800-638-3775

Teach Three-Part Reading Comprehension Lessons

In guiding children's reading to improve comprehension, part of your teaching role is to carefully design supports to account for what happens before, during, and after the reading of a text. Before students read, help them build background knowledge related to the content and structure of the text. You may engage students by reminding them of the elements of a typical story or by talking about the illustrations of a story to be read. You might ask students to predict what is going to happen in a story, or ask students what they might learn from a nonfiction passage. Ultimately, you help students establish a purpose for their reading.

During reading, provide the level of support each student needs to successfully address the purpose for reading. You might have the class chorally read or ask students to partner with a classmate and take turns reading. You can form cooperative learning groups with one member responsible for reading aloud to the small group. Be sure to include a few capable readers as performance models.

After reading, remind students of the purpose for reading, and guide students to reflect on the reading purpose. Guide students in discussing the text. Ask open-ended questions, and encourage student conversations with one another. Prompt students to explain reading strategies with questions such as, "How did you know that?" and "Where does it say that in the text?" Consider engaging students in related art, cooking, drama, music, or writing activities, not as busywork but rather to facilitate deeper processing of important ideas they have read.

Quick-Guides to Inclusion 3: Ideas for Educating Students with Disabilities © Michael F. Giangreco 2002
Available through Paul H. Brookes Publishing Co., Baltimore: 1-800-638-3775

#8

Use a Word Wall

Use a Word Wall

Word walls help students learn to read and spell words accurately and automatically. They are literally entire classroom walls with five words added each week, arranged alphabetically by first letter (see Figure 1). Students may use a manila folder as their word wall or a communication device with the words programmed accordingly. Whatever physical format is required to make the wall accessible to students, the wall provides a support for students in spelling and reading words that students encounter across the day. Over the course of a year, a word wall helps students learn 125 or more sight words and dozens of strategies to spell and read unfamiliar words.

Like any strategy, it isn't effective if it isn't used thoughtfully. The wall includes words that occur frequently in text, have common spelling patterns, or are meaningful in the classroom culture (e.g., "Quidditch" from Harry Potter). The shape of words is outlined, and a color background provides visual cues. Words remain on the wall all year, and children learn to use the wall in reading and spelling throughout the day. Word wall instruction encourages students to look carefully at spelling patterns and provides ongoing, varied repetition of all the words while emphasizing the new words each week.

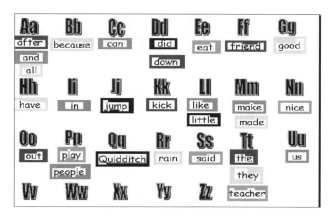

Figure 1.   An example of a word wall after several weeks of school.

Quick-Guides to Inclusion 3: Ideas for Educating Students with Disabilities © Michael F. Giangreco 2002
Available through Paul H. Brookes Publishing Co., Baltimore: 1-800-638-3775

#9

Teach the Writing Process

Teach the Writing Process

Writing is a complex act—essentially, thinking on paper. To write effectively, students must think simultaneously on multiple levels about the ideas they want to convey; what knowledge their audience already has about their message; word choice, grammar and spelling rules; and more. Students must learn individual skills as well as the ability to juggle these skills in fluent writing.

To learn to write, children must first generate a text. This can be done by dictating a message to a scribe, handwriting, typing, or using a variety of alternative keyboards and software. Be sure to respond to students' texts as meaningful, even, or especially, when the meaningfulness is not obvious to you. For example, children may scribble, combine pictures and apparently random letters, or spell words unconventionally. Being genuinely interested in the student's message is one of the most powerful motivators of conventional spelling or grammar. An "author's chair," where children read aloud what they have written, is one way to encourage a developing writer's motivation and attention.

Two strategies are especially helpful to teach specific skills and assist individual children: classwide mini-lessons and individual student conferences. Mini-lessons, 5–10 minutes in length, are used to teach a new writing rule or strategy. You can present examples and nonexamples of the rule, model thinking strategies, or use the newly learned rule to revise an anonymous student's writing from the previous year's class. Teachers hold individual conferences with a few students each day to monitor progress, interests, relative strengths, and needs.

Quick-Guides to Inclusion 3: Ideas for Educating Students with Disabilities © Michael F. Giangreco 2002
Available through Paul H. Brookes Publishing Co., Baltimore: 1-800-638-3775

#10

Perfect Practice
Makes Perfect

Perfect Practice Makes Perfect

Practice makes perfect. Your parents, coaches, chorus directors, and teachers have repeated that mantra each time you complained during the struggles of learning a new skill until it has played like a tune in your head. You probably have said it to your own students.

For a few gifted performers, practice does make perfect: Larry Bird's jump shot, a Robin Williams monologue, a Frank Lloyd Wright design, a Bobby McFerrin solo, or my grandmother's Italian soup.

Most of us, however, never achieve perfection despite hours, days, or even years of practice. Some of us lose interest and quit. Many of us become frustrated and avoid particular activities the rest of our lives.

The key to maximizing practice time is to focus on perfect practice. That is, students need to practice skills accurately and well in order to develop fluency. In reading books, one way that you can aim for perfection is by asking a struggling reader to read along with an audiotaped book. You might use a small set of letters with struggling spellers and guide their spelling of words using just those letters (e.g., e, i, l, n, s, t to spell l, it, is, in, tin, sin, sit, site, list, listen).

Choose seatwork or homework tasks that require students to practice skills already learned in class rather than new tasks. The goal is to increase student success, reduce frustration, and increase the odds that what students learn through practice is accurate and, ultimately, automatic.

Quick-Guides to Inclusion 3: Ideas for Educating Students with Disabilities © Michael F. Giangreco 2002
Available through Paul H. Brookes Publishing Co., Baltimore: 1-800-638-3775

Selected References

Allington, R.L. (2001). *What really matters for struggling readers: Designing research-based programs.* New York: Longman.

Cunningham, P.M., Hall, D.P., & Sigmon, C.M. (1999). *The teacher's guide to the four blocks.* Greensboro, NC: Carson-Dellosa.

Erickson, K.A., & Koppenhaver, D.A. (1998). Using the "write talk-nology" with Patrik. *Teaching Exceptional Children, 31*(1), 58–64.

Keefe, C.H. (1996). *Label-free learning: Supporting learners with disabilities.* York, ME: Stenhouse.

Male, M. (1996). *Technology for inclusion: Meeting the special needs of all students* (3rd ed.). Needham Heights, MA: Allyn & Bacon.

Musselwhite, C., & King-DeBaun, P. (1997). *Emergent literacy success: Merging technology and whole language for students with disabilities.* Litchfield Park, AZ: Special Communications.

Rhodes, L.K. (1996). *Readers and writers with a difference: A holistic approach to teaching struggling readers and writers.* Portsmouth, NH: Heinemann.

Taberski, S. (2000). *On solid ground.* Portsmouth, NH: Heinemann.

Quick-Guides to Inclusion 3: Ideas for Educating Students with Disabilities © Michael F. Giangreco 2002
Available through Paul H. Brookes Publishing Co., Baltimore: 1-800-638-3775

Quick-Guide #13

Supporting Friendships For All Students

Carol Tashie and Zach Rossetti

Quick-Guides to Inclusion 3:
Ideas for Educating Students with Disabilities

Michael F. Giangreco
Series Editor

Dear Teacher,

So much of school is about memorable experiences with people: great teachers, good friends, boyfriends, girlfriends, "just friends," and ex-friends. Sure, students learn about history and math and English, but even more so, students learn about friendship, diversity, and loyalty. Through their participation in classes and clubs and teams and committees, students develop relationships. Through these relationships, students learn a great deal about getting along with other people—now and in the future.

All students need a wide variety of relationships with their classmates. Not everyone will have an honor roll grade-point average, be the captain of the team, or have the lead in the school play; but everyone can make friends. Unfortunately, many students with disabilities do not have friends. Far too often, they spend the bulk of their school days surrounded by adults. Many parents of students with disabilities report that their children are lonely, with only the television, other family members, or paid adults to keep them company after school. The telephone never rings; no one comes to visit.

As a teacher, you may encounter students who face the world pretty much alone. You may wonder what you can do to respect the need for belonging that all students feel. What follows are suggestions on how to support students to develop meaningful and reciprocal relationships with others in their lives. We encourage you to view these connections as important and crucial parts of every student's education.

Peace,

Carol and Zach

GUIDELINES-AT-A-GLANCE

1. Everyone Can and Should Have Friends

2. Model the Highest Expectations for All Students

3. Make Sure All Students Share Time, Space, and Activities

4. Not Being Able to Speak Is Not the Same as Having Nothing to Say

5. Create a Class that Truly Celebrates, Not Simply Tolerates, Diversity

6. Don't Get in the Way—Respect the Space that Friendships Require

7. Recognize the Single Most Underutilized Resource in Schools: Students

8. You Can't Do it Alone—Families Are Essential

9. Pay Attention to What Friendship Is and Isn't

10. Provide Intentional Facilitation

Quick-Guides to Inclusion 3: Ideas for Educating Students with Disabilities © Michael F. Giangreco 2002
Available through Paul H. Brookes Publishing Co., Baltimore: 1-800-638-3775

#1

Everyone Can and Should Have Friends

Everyone Can and Should Have Friends

Over the last few years, we have discovered a great deal about friendships between students with and without disabilities. From talking to students and listening to their stories, we have learned that all students can develop meaningful friendships. We also have learned that friendships are more likely to occur when all of the people in a student's life truly believe that she is someone who would make a great friend.

As a classroom teacher, you have the opportunity to create environments and conditions that foster relationships between all students. You can begin the school year by having all students participate in "get acquainted" activities. These activities give students the opportunities to get to know their classmates in fun and memorable ways. You can structure cooperative learning lessons, affirming the notions of interdependence and the power of students working together. Learning centers and other small-group situations develop social bonds as students teach and learn from one another. Even when students are working independently, teachers can encourage student connections by allowing them to ask each other for help, proofread first drafts, and brainstorm ideas with each other. These kinds of classroom strategies can provide the foundation for the development of meaningful and reciprocal friendships.

This foundation may be solid enough to support relationships for many students. For other students, teachers will need to work closely with team members to develop and implement individual plans for the active facilitation of friendships. The following pages offer further guidelines to assist in developing these plans.

Quick-Guides to Inclusion 3: Ideas for Educating Students with Disabilities © Michael F. Giangreco 2002
Available through Paul H. Brookes Publishing Co., Baltimore: 1-800-638-3775

#2

Model the Highest Expectations for All Students

Model the Highest Expectations for All Students

The ways in which students are regarded by their classmates are strongly influenced by how they are perceived by their teachers. Therefore, the likelihood that friendships will develop increases when you consider and treat all of your students as valued, capable, and interesting individuals. When students with disabilities are consistently characterized by their labels (e.g., "the Down syndrome student") or spoken to as if they don't understand, it is less likely that classmates will take the time to look past the label and get to know the person. Because children observe and internalize much of what adults do, these messages can convey to classmates that the student is "not worth knowing." This can build formidable barriers to friendship.

To avoid or overcome these barriers, you can be a role model for your students and the other adults in your school. Through respectful language (e.g., describing Shaffer as someone who loves lacrosse and the Grateful Dead), you can model for others that the student with disabilities is a "person first." You can show your students, through your actions and words, that you believe they all possess the potential to be successful and live the lives they wish to lead. By talking to and about the student in ways consistent with his chronological age, you model age-appropriate expectations. When you make modifications to curriculum only when necessary and are always respectful of the student's gifts, learning style, and grade level, other students will be able to view him as a contributing and integral member of the class. When you demonstrate your belief that the student with disabilities is not deficient but simply moves through the world in different ways, you teach your students that the student with disabilities is not "broken," does not need to be "fixed," and has much to contribute as a student and as a friend.

Quick-Guides to Inclusion 3: Ideas for Educating Students with Disabilities © Michael F. Giangreco 2002
Available through Paul H. Brookes Publishing Co., Baltimore: 1-800-638-3775

#3

Make Sure All Students Share Time, Space, and Activities

Make Sure All Students Share Time, Space, and Activities

Students need to be together to develop respect, mutual interests, and real friendships. Classrooms provide all students with the opportunities to share experiences and appreciate each other's company. Great classrooms offer students planned and spontaneous chances to learn together and connect socially. However, for too many students with disabilities, even those who are in general education classes, their school days still consist of separate places and lessons. Far too many students with disabilities continue to be "pulled out" of their classrooms to receive services from therapists and special educators. This practice, besides having questionable educational value, significantly impacts the student's ability to make friends. The student who leaves the classroom misses important opportunities to connect with classmates around content, knowledge, and activities.

As a teacher, you can reject the notion that some students must leave the classroom in order to learn. You have the power to develop a classroom environment that allows each student to participate in and learn from all lessons. For example, when teaching a history lesson on World War II, you can provide students different ways to develop and demonstrate their knowledge. Some students may write a journal in the style of Anne Frank, others can create a mural representing the treaty at Yalta, whereas still others may develop a game of Jeopardy! in which all students can participate as hosts, card-turners, or contestants. Teaching with this emphasis on different learning styles recognizes that all students can learn and that we value the ways in which they do. By supporting meaningful learning outcomes for all students, teachers can send the clear message that a disability need not be a "handicap" to learning, ability, or friendship.

Quick-Guides to Inclusion 3: Ideas for Educating Students with Disabilities © Michael F. Giangreco 2002
Available through Paul H. Brookes Publishing Co., Baltimore: 1-800-638-3775

#4

Not Being
Able to Speak Is
Not the Same as
Having Nothing to Say

Quick-Guides to Inclusion 3: Ideas for Educating Students with Disabilities © Michael F. Giangreco 2002
Available through Paul H. Brookes Publishing Co., Baltimore: 1-800-638-3775

Not Being Able to Speak Is Not the Same as Having Nothing to Say

For too long, people believed that students who did not speak or speak easily did not have very much to say. Assumptions about students' abilities, comprehension, and even interests were made based on archaic views of intelligence and capability. However, the advent of various forms of augmentative and alternative communication (AAC) has allowed many people, once labeled "mentally retarded" because they could not fully express themselves, to communicate their intelligence, wit, and personalities.

We also know that even when students are not yet able to express all they know, they are still communicating. Whether through body language, facial expressions, behaviors, or gestures, everyone communicates. It is up to us to "learn to listen" to what they are saying. And when we believe that every student has something to say, we can tap into the resources of AAC to "augment" their ability to communicate knowledge, thoughts, and desires.

Supporting a student's ability to communicate is critical to developing social relationships. Although having a sophisticated means of communication is not a prerequisite for friendship, it does assist students in getting to know each other more easily. An effective starting point is to ask families and classmates about the ways in which a student currently communicates and what other things she may want to say. If a student uses a communication device, classmates can suggest words to include, based on what students her age talk about. As the teacher, you are also key to making sure a student's communication device is always within her reach and that all other students understand how and why it is used. It is important to let students know about all of the ways a student communicates; when students know how to communicate with each other, they usually do.

Quick-Guides to Inclusion 3: Ideas for Educating Students with Disabilities © Michael F. Giangreco 2002
Available through Paul H. Brookes Publishing Co., Baltimore: 1-800-638-3775

#5

Create a Class that Truly Celebrates, Not Simply Tolerates, Diversity

---

Create a Class that Truly Celebrates, Not Simply Tolerates, Diversity

It is not enough for schools to simply "tolerate" the differences among us, for tolerance implies a hierarchy of value. One prizes *good* health but *tolerates* a cold. When schools promote tolerance, they send the message to students that "you are welcome only if you act, look, sound, think, and talk like us." This reinforces the prejudice of a social hierarchy, decreasing the likelihood that students will become friends. Yet, when schools strive to "celebrate" diversity, they send the message to all students, "you are welcome as you are."

To create a classroom that celebrates diversity, many teachers have found it useful to embed the contributions of people with disabilities into their lessons. When studying inventors, teachers highlight Temple Grandin, a woman with autism who invented livestock management techniques. When choosing literature, teachers can introduce *Stuck in Neutral* (Trueman, 2000), a book about a teenager who has cerebral palsy. When teaching about civil rights, teachers can include the contributions of Ed Roberts to the independent living movement and the 1988 student protest at Gallaudet University. Teachers can teach that many of the most influential people in history have had disabilities, including Franklin Delano Roosevelt. In addition, they can teach that many important inventions, such as the telephone (invented by Alexander Graham Bell), were invented to support people with disabilities. By including people with disabilities as integral parts of the curriculum, teachers create classrooms that truly celebrate the contributions of everyone. When the abilities of each student are equally celebrated, students learn to appreciate their own and each other's gifts. They gain confidence and the true sense of belonging.

Quick-Guides to Inclusion 3: Ideas for Educating Students with Disabilities © Michael F. Giangreco 2002
Available through Paul H. Brookes Publishing Co., Baltimore: 1–800–638–3775

#6

Don't Get in the Way—Respect the Space that Friendships Require

---

Quick-Guides to Inclusion 3: Ideas for Educating Students with Disabilities © Michael F. Giangreco 2002
Available through Paul H. Brookes Publishing Co., Baltimore: 1-800-638-3775

Don't Get in the Way—Respect the Space that Friendships Require

When students were asked why no one ate lunch with Esther, her teachers expected to hear complaints of personal eating habits or difficulty with communication. Instead, they got an earful: no one eats with Esther because no one wants to sit with the adult who is always by Esther's side. For many students with disabilities, their independence is inadvertently stifled by the presence of a paraprofessional. Although a paraprofessional's role can be extremely useful in providing educational support, it can also act as a barrier, literally, to students' developing relationships with classmates.

As a classroom teacher, you can ensure that a paraprofessional working in your classroom understands her role in supporting students both educationally and socially. You can help the paraprofessional understand the importance of social relationships and the potential of all students as friends. You can support the paraprofessional in encouraging social relationships by helping students take advantage of naturally occurring opportunities to interact. Based on your collective knowledge of the student, you can encourage students to recognize their common interests, hobbies, and passions. Together, you can provide information to other students about the ways in which a student expresses herself and can brainstorm ideas with students about how she can participate in school and after-school events.

The role of the paraprofessional is to support you to be a great teacher to all students in your class. You can let the paraprofessional know that you see the student with disabilities as "one of your students," and you do not want her to sit too closely to the student, talk for her, or stand in the way of "kids being kids." Together, you can set the stage for friendship and then sit back as the magic unfolds.

Quick-Guides to Inclusion 3: Ideas for Educating Students with Disabilities © Michael F. Giangreco 2002
Available through Paul H. Brookes Publishing Co., Baltimore: 1-800-638-3775

#7

Recognize the Single
Most Underutilized
Resource in Schools:
Students

Recognize the Single Most Underutilized Resource in Schools: Students

As every teacher knows, students are not just learners, they are valuable teachers of everything from helping classmates learn new skills to creating classroom rules. Similarly, students can be incredible resources to help teams understand ways to support a student to become more connected with his classmates. Following these two basic guidelines will serve you well: *Ask* students to tell you what *you* need to know. *Tell* the students what *they* need to know.

Students can give you information about what friendship is like for students their age. They can tell you how they meet, where they go, and why they like to hang out together. They can inform you about opportunities for social connections and let you know what students with particular interests do when they get together. Students can advise you on whom a student may want to spend time with and can serve as inside connectors to introduce one student to another or to a group. They can tell you when adults should step in and when they should bow out. Many teams believe so strongly in the value of the information that students can supply that they regularly invite classmates to participate in student meetings.

In addition to asking students' advice, it is also important to provide students with the information they require to better connect with their classmates. In order for students to become friends, they need to understand everything from how that person communicates and the ways in which he requires support to what his passions are and what drives him crazy. No adult can truly know what it is like to be a student. Luckily, teachers have easy access to the real experts—the students.

Quick-Guides to Inclusion 3: Ideas for Educating Students with Disabilities © Michael F. Giangreco 2002
Available through Paul H. Brookes Publishing Co., Baltimore: 1–800–638–3775

#8

You Can't Do it Alone— Families Are Essential

Quick-Guides to Inclusion 3: Ideas for Educating Students with Disabilities © Michael F. Giangreco 2002
Available through Paul H. Brookes Publishing Co., Baltimore: 1-800-638-3775

You Can't Do it Alone— Families Are Essential

Open and honest communication between families and schools is key to the collaboration that is required to support all students to have meaningful relationships. It may be helpful to follow two basic guidelines with families: 1) *Ask* families to tell you what they believe, desire, and require; and 2) *inform* families what you know, need to learn, and hope to accomplish.

Families know their children best and are invaluable resources when trying to understand a student's interests and gifts. Families can provide information about the things their children do at home, which may translate into how a student can get involved in school. Families can also provide a historical perspective, such as which classmates a student has known for years and ways in which relationships were developed in earlier grades.

It is crucial to recognize and respect that the risk taking that friendship involves can be difficult for some families. A useful strategy is to ask families about their "nonnegotiables." What are the things that they cannot ignore, compromise, or alter, no matter what the cost? For example, one family did not want their daughter to eat out with friends. When it was understood that their nonnegotiable was the student's macrobiotic diet, the issue was resolved by providing her friends with a list of foods she could and could not eat. Once nonnegotiables are on the table, collaboration becomes more effective and less stressful for all involved.

It is also helpful to give families information about friendship. Teachers can give families ideas of which students share their child's interests, schedules of school and nonschool sponsored activities, and ideas for carpools. Schools can help families connect with other students who can offer valuable information about the ins and outs of friendship.

Quick-Guides to Inclusion 3: Ideas for Educating Students with Disabilities © Michael F. Giangreco 2002
Available through Paul H. Brookes Publishing Co., Baltimore: 1-800-638-3775

#9

Pay Attention to What Friendship Is and Isn't

Pay Attention to What Friendship Is and Isn't

In third grade, Kevin's team developed a "buddy list" so that he would always have someone to play with at recess. The team was surprised that Kevin was not happy at recess, except every tenth day when Trey was his assigned buddy. The teacher quickly realized that Kevin did not want a rotation of classmates, he wanted a friend. She took down the buddy list and began supporting the budding relationship between Kevin and Trey.

In the quest to help students develop relationships with others their age, many people use strategies such as buddy lists or "circles of friends." Although done with good intentions, these strategies often perpetuate the notion that students with disabilities cannot have true friends, and being with an assigned buddy is the best they can do.

As a teacher, you are in the unique position to support the development of true friendships. You can see which students have a natural affinity to each other and can encourage ways for those students to get to know each other better. You can group these students together to learn cooperatively through lessons, to work on the class bulletin board, and to play on the same dodge ball team at recess. If you do not see these relationships extending beyond the classroom, then you can have conversations with students to find out what questions they have and what supports and information they need. You can also pay attention to the natural places and ways that your students interact. If, for example, students play in the sand box at recess, then you can encourage the student's parent to send in cool toys to share with classmates. If students play card games at snack time, then you can make sure the student is in the middle of the action. The key is to pay attention to what friendship really is for all kids and not be fooled by what it isn't.

Quick-Guides to Inclusion 3: Ideas for Educating Students with Disabilities © Michael F. Giangreco 2002
Available through Paul H. Brookes Publishing Co., Baltimore: 1–800–638–3775

#10

Provide
Intentional Facilitation

Provide Intentional Facilitation

Hopefully, the nine guidelines you have read so far have given you ideas on how to create class and school environments that provide fertile ground for friendships to grow. However, for some students, it may be necessary to provide intentional facilitation of friendship. Although it sounds formal, *intentional facilitation* is simply the process of getting to know the student and then supporting her to become better connected. The person who provides intentional facilitation should be well-versed with the nine guidelines previously described and be able to confidently convey these values to others. This person should be someone with whom the student is comfortable and who strongly respects her gifts. For older students, the facilitator can be someone close to the student's own age. Although this person will lead the process, he must recognize that it is a cooperative effort, involving the student, family, school, and classmates.

The process begins by getting to know the student and others her age. Ways to gather this information include conversations with and observations of the student; conversations with classmates, families, and teachers; and the use of formal processes such as Making Action Plans (MAPS; O'Brien, Forest, Snow, & Hasbury, 1989). Information on what friendships look like for all students this age, as well as an understanding of what is typically available in the school and the neighborhood for students with similar interests, is essential. Once this is all gathered, the facilitator can begin to connect the student with people, clubs, and events that match the student's desires.

Intentional facilitation is not magic—it is the deliberate connection of one student with others who may share her passions and interests. However, when done right, it can unleash the real magic of friendship.

*Quick-Guides to Inclusion 3: Ideas for Educating Students with Disabilities © Michael F. Giangreco 2002
Available through Paul H. Brookes Publishing Co., Baltimore: 1-800-638-3775*

Selected References

Biklen, D., & Duchan, J.F. (1994). "I am intelligent": The social construction of mental retardation. *Journal of The Association for Persons with Severe Handicaps, 19,* 173–184.

Crossley, R. (1997). *Speechless: Facilitating communication for people without voices.* New York: Dutton.

Donnellan, A.M., & Leary, M.R. (1995). *Movement differences and diversity in autism and mental retardation.* Madison, WI: DRI Press.

O'Brien, J., Forest, M., Snow, J., & Hasbury, D. (1989). *Action for inclusion.* Toronto: Frontier College Press.

Lovett, H. (1996). *Learning to listen: Positive approaches and people with difficult behavior.* Baltimore: Paul H. Brookes Publishing Co.

Rossetti, Z.S., & Tashie, C.Z. (2000). *The process for facilitating social relationships.* Durham, NH: Institute on Disability.

Sapon-Shevin, M. (1999). *Because we can change the world.* Needham Heights, MA: Allyn & Bacon.

Shapiro, J.P. (1994). *No pity.* New York: Times Books.

Strully, J.L., & Strully, C.F. (1989). Friendships as an educational goal. In S. Stainback, W. Stainback, & M. Forest (Eds.), *Educating all students in the mainstream of regular education* (pp. 59–68). Baltimore: Paul H. Brookes Publishing Co.

Trueman, T. (2000). *Stuck in neutral.* New York: HarperCollins.

Van der Klift, E., & Kunc, N. (1994). Beyond benevolence: Friendship and the politics of help. In J.S. Thousand, R.A. Villa, & A.I. Nevin (Eds.), *Creativity and collaborative learning: A practical guide to empowering students and teachers* (pp. 391–401). Baltimore: Paul H. Brookes Publishing Co.

Quick-Guides to Inclusion 3: Ideas for Educating Students with Disabilities © Michael F. Giangreco 2002
Available through Paul H. Brookes Publishing Co., Baltimore: 1-800-638-3775

Quick Guide #14

Self-Determination

Michael L. Wehmeyer

Quick-Guides to Inclusion 3:
Ideas for Educating Students with Disabilities

Michael F. Giangreco
Series Editor

Dear Teacher,

In the course of your teaching career, have you met students who you just knew would be successful? These students have goals and plans to achieve them. They can identify barriers to success and find solutions to remove them. They know what they are good at and capitalize on their strengths. These students are self-determined. They take charge of their own learning, work toward self-set goals, and are ready when opportunity comes knocking! Ever wish you could bottle whatever it is that the self-determined student has and inoculate all your students with it? Of course, nothing in education is ever as easy as just giving a shot, but you can ensure that your students have the opportunity to become more self-determined.

Promoting self-determination is important for all students. It is never too early or too late to teach students the skills that will enable them to become more self-determined. Chances are, there are learning standards in your school for all students to achieve that reflect self-determination skills such as problem solving, decision making, or goal setting. Too often, students with disabilities have not had the opportunity to learn self-determination skills as a part of their curriculum. That's what this Quick-Guide is about. When students learn self-determination skills, they can take more responsibility for directing their own learning and become less dependent on others. Promoting self-determination provides a useful strategy to enhance inclusion in general education and help students with disabilities lead more personally fulfilling lives.

Good Luck!

Mike

GUIDELINES-AT-A-GLANCE

1. It Starts with Your Example:
   Model Problem Solving

2. Tell Students You Believe They
   Are Capable

3. Emphasize Student Strengths
   and Uniqueness

4. Create a Learning Community that
   Promotes Risk Taking

5. Structure Your Classroom to Promote
   Choice Making

6. Empower Students to Make Decisions
   and Set Goals

7. Teach Students Self-Determination Skills

8. Encourage Student-Directed Learning

9. Use Peers to Provide Supports

10. Advocate for Your Own Self-Determination

Quick-Guides to Inclusion 3: Ideas for Educating Students with Disabilities © Michael F. Giangreco 2002
Available through Paul H. Brookes Publishing Co., Baltimore: 1-800-638-3775

#1

It Starts with
Your Example:
Model Problem Solving

It Starts with Your Example: Model Problem Solving

A *problem* is an event or task for which a solution is not readily known. If you think about it, life is full of problems that one must solve and keep solving. Not just big problems, such as how to pay the rent or put food on the table, but everyday problems, such as what to do when your child is sick and can't go to school but both parents have work deadlines or how to get gum out of the carpet! Many problems are social in nature, involving problems in relationships and peer interactions. *Problem solving* is a process of identifying one or more solutions to a problem and taking action.

How can you teach problem solving? The curriculum in most states includes standards across multiple grade levels and content domains that address students' acquisition of problem-solving skills. Students can be taught how to identify and generate solutions to a problem. As students get older, they should be provided opportunities to solve increasingly complex problems and to apply their growing problem-solving skills in making decisions about their lives. Students with disabilities, like all students, need such instruction and can acquire better problem-solving skills.

Perhaps as important, however, you need to model the problem-solving process you apply to solve the problems that confront you every day. Most adults apply problem-solving approaches to situations but don't usually verbalize them. What do you do when you turn on the overhead projector and the light bulb goes out? Instead of just solving the problem, communicate the steps of your problem-solving process to students as you engage in the process. Believe it or not, they really do watch what you do and learn from you!

Quick-Guides to Inclusion 3: Ideas for Educating Students with Disabilities © Michael F. Giangreco 2002
Available through Paul H. Brookes Publishing Co., Baltimore: 1–800–638–3775

#2

Tell Students
You Believe They
Are Capable

Tell Students
You Believe They Are Capable

It is important to focus on skill development and knowledge attainment to promote self-determination. Certainly, teaching students skills such as problem solving, decision making, goal setting, or self-direction are critical components of your role in enhancing student self-determination. However, it is not enough *just* to teach these skills. Ability is of little value without opportunity. Opportunity is important because not only do you get the chance to practice new skills and refine longer-held skills, but you begin to believe that you are capable and can make things happen in your life.

At its core, self-determination is about making things happen in your life. Even people with limited decision-making or problem-solving skills can make things happen in their lives. Most people can almost always figure out ways to get around skill or knowledge limitations. Those who can't do math can use an accountant to do their taxes. Those who can't read can use a text reader. You get the point. Learning skills is important, but we can make accommodations for situations when students don't possess important skills.

When students don't believe they are capable or can overcome barriers in their way to achievement, however, we can't just accommodate with technology. Students come to believe that they are capable and can overcome barriers through opportunities to learn and practice skills related to self-determination— by succeeding in tasks and by being told by adults in their lives that they are capable, competent, and valued individuals. Saying, "I believe in you" might be more important than anything else you do. Do it often and with conviction!

Quick-Guides to Inclusion 3: Ideas for Educating Students with Disabilities © Michael F. Giangreco 2002
Available through Paul H. Brookes Publishing Co., Baltimore: 1-800-638-3775

#3

Emphasize Student Strengths and Uniqueness

Emphasize Student Strengths and Uniqueness

Historically, special education has had a deficit focus. That is, the emphasis in educational services and programming has been on identifying perceived student deficits and providing instruction to, in some sense, "fix" the deficit. It is not unusual for students with disabilities to have a broad and expansive knowledge about what they do not do well and about their problems yet not be able to tell you a single thing about what they do well. Students with disabilities have, almost universally, experienced failure in the school system. The very process that students go through to receive special education supports begins with student failure in one or more academic areas. Educational meetings that set goals about the student's individualized education often begin with a litany of what the student cannot do.

It goes without saying that this focus on *deficit* and *disability* does not lend itself to convincing students they are capable, competent, and valued individuals. When the education process focuses only on what the student can't do, it increases the likelihood that the student will perform up to expectations—low expectations, that is. One consistent finding in the education literature is that students achieve what teachers expect them to achieve. As you plan your lessons and units and implement instruction for your students, it is important to think about each student's abilities and uniqueness and to build on those. Students need to learn that everyone is unique and learns differently. Students with disabilities need to learn that they may have unique learning needs but that those needs can be met and are balanced by the student's abilities.

Quick-Guides to Inclusion 3: Ideas for Educating Students with Disabilities © Michael F. Giangreco 2002
Available through Paul H. Brookes Publishing Co., Baltimore: 1-800-638-3775

#4

Create a Learning Community that Promotes Risk Taking

Create a Learning Community that Promotes Risk Taking

One way to meet the needs of students with diverse learning, language, cultural, and economic characteristics is to create learning communities that respect—indeed celebrate—this diversity. *Learning communities* are intentionally created environments in which students learn to respect individual differences, work in a self-directed manner, apply problem-solving and decision-making strategies to educational problems, and participate in setting classroom rules. Teachers who create learning communities do so by gaining knowledge about the abilities of all their students; developing systematic ways to collect meaningful information on student progress to plan future lessons; using collaborative teaching, grouping, and differentiated instruction to individualize student educational experiences; and taking on the roles of coach and facilitator as well as instructor.

Creating such learning communities is critical to promoting self-determination. In such settings, students learn they have a voice in the educational process by their participation in rule setting. They learn about other students and their unique abilities and needs and to solve social problems through mediation or conflict resolution processes. Perhaps most importantly, they learn they can take risks. Learning to solve problems, make decisions, and set goals can only be accomplished by taking risks. When students feel that they will be ridiculed or punished for failing, they don't take such risks. Intentional learning communities support and even value risk taking and, in turn, teach students that failure is not an end but a means to success and, in the end, promotes self-determination!

Quick-Guides to Inclusion 3: Ideas for Educating Students with Disabilities © Michael F. Giangreco 2002
Available through Paul H. Brookes Publishing Co., Baltimore: 1-800-638-3775

#5

Structure
Your Classroom to
Promote Choice Making

Quick-Guides to Inclusion 3: Ideas for Educating Students with Disabilities © Michael F. Giangreco 2002
Available through Paul H. Brookes Publishing Co., Baltimore: 1-800-638-3775

Structure Your Classroom to Promote Choice Making

One of the best ways to teach students that they can make things happen in their lives is to provide them with numerous opportunities to make choices. A *choice* is simply communicating a preference between two or more options. Unlike goal setting, decision making, or problem solving, we rarely have to teach students how to make a choice. True, some students with more significant learning needs may need to be taught how to more effectively communicate their preferences, but for the most part, students come to school with a lot of preferences and are perfectly willing to tell you about them!

Believe it or not, this works to your advantage in promoting self-determination. If you structure your classroom to maximize the opportunity for students of all ages to make choices, then you are creating an environment in which students will learn that their opinions and preferences are valued. Moreover, many younger children (and for that matter, older students) need to learn that not every option is available to them, even if they prefer it! There are many ways to infuse choice into instruction, such as letting students choose where or with whom they perform an activity, when they work on a task, when they begin or end a task, and so forth. Even when what the student must learn is dictated to the student, as much of the curriculum is, you can create choice opportunities by offering different ways to learn the same information or material.

Quick-Guides to Inclusion 3: Ideas for Educating Students with Disabilities © Michael F. Giangreco 2002
Available through Paul H. Brookes Publishing Co., Baltimore: 1-800-638-3775

#6

Empower Students to Make Decisions and Set Goals

Empower Students to Make Decisions and Set Goals

Empowerment is a term usually associated with social movements and used in reference to actions that enable people to control their own lives. To empower a student is to enable that student to exert control and make things happen for himself. The verb *enable* is used purposefully, for we usually *do* things "to" or "for" students. Instead, we need to serve as catalysts to ensure that students have the chance to take some control over their lives, to provide support to that student when she is unsure about her capacity to make something happen, and to create the circumstances under which a student can exert control.

The educational process is goal oriented, and there is no better way to empower students to exert control than to actively involve them in setting goals about their instruction. The word *involve* comes from the Latin word *involvere*, which means to enwrap or entwine. We need to get students enwrapped in their education by enabling them to set goals and by supporting them in making decisions about their education and their lives. This may mean that you teach them how to set goals or how to make decisions. However, we must *go beyond* simply teaching skills and doing things to or for a student. Students need opportunities to exercise their skills to set goals and make decisions that impact their lives.

Students with disabilities are particularly prone to having others make decisions about them and set goals for them. In many ways, the special education process creates dependency. Involve all students in the educational decision-making process. Enable them to set goals that are meaningful to them. In so doing, you empower them for life.

Quick-Guides to Inclusion 3: Ideas for Educating Students with Disabilities © Michael F. Giangreco 2002
Available through Paul H. Brookes Publishing Co., Baltimore: 1-800-638-3775

#7

Teach Students Self-Determination Skills

Teach Students Self-Determination Skills

Learning skills to become more self-determined helps students to be more self-reliant. There is a wide array of skills and knowledge related to self-determination that students need to learn. Problem-solving, decision-making, and goal-setting skills have already been mentioned in previous guides. In addition, students need to learn to self-regulate learning and self-manage their lives—a focus discussed in a subsequent guideline. There are still other important areas, however. Students need to learn how to become self-advocates—how to stand up for their rights and advocate on their own behalf. To do so, they will need to learn some effective communication skills, how to negotiate and compromise, or how to use persuasion. They will need to learn to listen as well as to speak or to communicate through nonverbal means.

Another important area is in the domain of self-awareness. The importance of emphasizing capacity and uniqueness has already been discussed, and this is particularly important in promoting self- and disability-awareness. The purpose of such activities is not to get the student to simply accept the label the school has assigned to that student but to explore areas of strengths and the unique needs the student needs to succeed. Like all students, young people with disabilities need friends. In addition, students with a disability can learn and grow from relationships with adult mentors who have a similar disability and whose life story will inform the students and encourage them to work toward self-reliance and self-sufficiency.

Quick-Guides to Inclusion 3: Ideas for Educating Students with Disabilities © Michael F. Giangreco 2002
Available through Paul H. Brookes Publishing Co., Baltimore: 1-800-638-3775

#8

Encourage Student-Directed Learning

Encourage Student-Directed Learning

School has been described (only slightly tongue-in-cheek) as a place where students have to go to do something someone else tells them to do. Most of what happens in schools is teacher- or other-directed. For example, traditional models of instruction have teachers setting instructional goals, identifying resources, providing instruction, evaluating student progress, and assigning grades. Although these teacher-directed activities are, in most cases, necessary, you can often turn over control to students by enabling them to do for themselves what you might otherwise do to or for them.

Take, for example, tracking progress of student goals. Typically, this responsibility is held exclusively by the teacher who records grades, scores papers, collects data on task completion, among other tasks. However, it is really quite easy to set up systems in which students are responsible for tracking their own progress on goals by graphing their progress, maintaining a log, or self-monitoring time on a task. Students with more significant disabilities may need highly individualized ways to track progress.

There are many ways we can enable students to self-direct learning. Teaching students problem-solving and goal-setting steps enables them to more effectively self-direct educational goal setting. You can provide students with pictures of a task in the correct sequence, which enables them to proceed without an adult prompting them. Materials can be available where all students can access them. The key is for you to look at what you do for students that they could do for themselves.

Quick-Guides to Inclusion 3: Ideas for Educating Students with Disabilities © Michael F. Giangreco 2002
Available through Paul H. Brookes Publishing Co., Baltimore: 1-800-638-3775

#9

Use Peers
to Provide Supports

Use Peers to Provide Supports

Another excellent way to promote self-determination is to link students with peers without disabilities in cooperative or collaborative learning groups. It seems to be the case that peers of the same age don't tend to do as much for or to students with disabilities and, instead, focus on supporting the student. It is likely that many teachers learned how to "let go" and let students with disabilities do things for themselves by watching how classmates interacted with the student! You should, of course, be cautious not to place peers without disabilities in roles that simply make them mini-teachers, and you also need to ensure that peers have ample opportunities to interact with the student as a classmate, potential friend, and fellow student. However, having a peer who is seated next to a student with a disability assist the student both provides support to the student needing assistance and creates an interaction and an opportunity to develop a friendship.

To say that peers are important for all children is to state the obvious, but it cannot be overstated that students with disabilities need to have chances to make friends with peers who don't have disabilities. Far too many children and adolescents with disabilities do not have frequent "play dates" with friends or get invited to birthday parties. Participation in the general classroom is the first step to promoting relationships with peers and encouraging friendships, but it is *only* the first step. You have to design the classroom so that peers without disabilities have an opportunity to get to know the student with a disability as a person first and not just as a person with a disability. Peers who begin providing supports and assistance may graduate to becoming the student's ally, advocate, and, hopefully, his friend.

Quick-Guides to Inclusion 3: Ideas for Educating Students with Disabilities © Michael F. Giangreco 2002
Available through Paul H. Brookes Publishing Co., Baltimore: 1-800-638-3775

#10

Advocate for Your Own Self-Determination

Advocate for Your Own Self-Determination

After reading the first nine guidelines, have you begun to wonder how you can turn control over to students to promote self-determination when you feel like everyone is telling you what to teach, how to teach, and what tests to give? If so, you are not alone. Too often, teachers feel they have less and less control over what and how they teach. Teachers' decisions can and do have an important effect on their students, and they are hesitant to give that up! It doesn't have to (and shouldn't) be that way, however. If educators are to effectively promote self-determination, then teachers must operate in environments that support their autonomy, respect their capacity, and promote their control over decisions that impact what they teach and how they teach it. In many states, teachers see the establishment of state educational standards and accountability testing as the embodiment of this lack of control.

What can you do? Become a self-advocate! Stand up for your right to have a voice in what is taught and how it is taught. Get on district committees that are adapting state standards to the local district, and fight to ensure that they are open ended and allow you the opportunity to work your magic and not just dictate that all students will perform the same task in the same way. Join professional organizations that are at the forefront of student self-determination, and become involved and informed. Get involved in research in which key stakeholders, such as students and teachers, have a voice in what research questions are asked. Become a leader in your district and on your campus, modeling effective practices and serving to train your colleagues. If you don't, nobody will do it for you!

*Quick-Guides to Inclusion 3: Ideas for Educating Students with Disabilities © Michael F. Giangreco 2002
Available through Paul H. Brookes Publishing Co., Baltimore: 1-800-638-3775*

Selected References

Field, S., & Hoffman, A. (1996). *Steps to self-determination.* Austin, TX: PRO-ED. (Available on-line at http://www.proedinc.com/)

Field, S., Hoffman, A., & Spezia, S. (1998). *Self-determination strategies for adolescents in transition.* Austin, TX: PRO-ED. (Available on-line at http://www.proedinc.com/)

Field, S., Martin, J., Miller, R., Ward, M., & Wehmeyer, M. (1998). *A practical guide to teaching self-determination.* Reston, VA: Council for Exceptional Children. (Available on-line at http://www.cec.sped.org/bk)

Halpern, A., Herr, C.M., Wolf, N.K., Doren, B., Johnson, M.D., & Lawson, J.D. (1997). *NEXT S.T.E.P.: Student transition and educational planning.* Austin, TX: PRO-ED. (Available on-line at http://www.proedinc.com/)

Martin, J.E., & Marshall, L.H. (1995). *ChoiceMaker: Self-Directed IEP.* Longmont, CO: Sopris West Publisher. (Available on-line at http://www.sopriswest.com/)

Wehmeyer, M.L., Agran, M., & Hughes, C. (1998). *Teaching self-determination to students with disabilities: Basic skills for successful transition.* Baltimore: Paul H. Brookes Publishing Co.

Wehmeyer, M.L., Palmer, S., Agran, M., Mithaug, D., & Martin, J. (2000). Promoting causal agency: The self-determined learning model of instruction. *Exceptional Children, 66,* 439–453.

Quick-Guide #15

Taking Inclusion to the Next Level: Creating Inclusive High School Classrooms

Cheryl M. Jorgensen, Douglas Fisher, and Carol Tashie

Quick-Guides to Inclusion 3:
Ideas for Educating Students with Disabilities

Michael F. Giangreco
Series Editor

Quick-Guides to Inclusion 3: Ideas for Educating Students with Disabilities © Michael F. Giangreco 2002
Available through Paul H. Brookes Publishing Co., Baltimore: 1–800–638–3775

Dear Teacher,

As a high school teacher, you have the power to shape a young person's future—an awesome responsibility but one that you have embraced. When a student with disabilities is enrolled in your class, you may wonder if you are prepared to meet this challenge. For most of us, neither our college education nor our past teaching experience provides a compass—some direction— particularly if the student has significant disabilities. This Quick-Guide is meant to remind you that the values and skills that make an effective teacher for students without disabilities are the very same ones that work for students with disabilities.

Before reading the 10 guidelines, take a little trip into the past. Think about your own high school experience. What were the most important things you learned in high school? Was it the Pythagorean theorem? Was it the Periodic Table of the Elements? More likely, it was a love of literature, good writing skills, how to drive a car, or getting along with people. You learned that you can act silly with your friends—but not in front of your boss. You learned how hard it is to stand up for what you believe in and disregard what the crowd thinks or does.

Which teachers do you remember with fondness and respect? It was probably the teachers who really loved teaching! They had high expectations and pushed you to do your best. They helped you see the relationship between what you were studying and your own life. These memorable and effective teachers understood that learning could be fun, and they strove to make the material "come alive" for students. They created a "family" atmosphere in their class—a place where you always felt welcome with no fear of rejection or judgment. And so it is for students with disabilities. Good inclusive teaching is not rocket science, but every teacher could use a roadmap. We hope that this Quick-Guide provides some direction for your exciting journey.

Sincerely,

Cheryl, Doug, and Carol

GUIDELINES-AT-A-GLANCE

1. Teach All High School Students Life's Most Important Lessons

2. Teach Students to Care About Learning by Caring About Them

3. Figure Out How Every Student Is "Smart"

4. Make Learning Relevant Through the Study of "Essential Questions"

5. Make Learning Cooperative

6. Allow Students a Variety of Ways to "Show What They Know"

7. When Students Need Intensive Supports, Provide Them as Naturally as Possible

8. Embed Social Justice Values in the Curriculum and Your Classroom

9. Become a Reflective Practitioner with Other Teachers in Your School

10. Advocate for Untracking and the Inclusion of All Students

Quick-Guides to Inclusion 3: Ideas for Educating Students with Disabilities © Michael F. Giangreco 2002
Available through Paul H. Brookes Publishing Co., Baltimore: 1-800-638-3775

#1

Teach All High School Students Life's Most Important Lessons

Teach All High School Students Life's Most Important Lessons

The "1-year rule" in education says that we should teach students what we want them to remember a year after the class is finished. To make sense of this rule, think about your students for a minute. Chances are, a year after the class ends, they will not remember all of the dates of the Civil War battles nor the exact formula for converting moles to grams (or is it grams to moles?). However, you might reasonably expect them to remember the economic significance of the Great Depression, the themes from *Romeo and Juliet* that carry over into modern times, and the negative impact of pollution on the environment. It is an even safer bet to assume that they will remember how their fear of reading Shakespeare dwindled with practice and success, the sense of satisfaction they felt when solving a difficult mathematical problem for the first time, and whether the concept of justice that they heard about in social studies class was practiced in their own school and community.

What does this 1-year rule have to do with teaching students with disabilities? It reminds us that memorization of facts and figures is by far the most fleeting—and least important—aspect of schooling. It tells us that all students—not just those who can easily recite back those memorized facts—can learn together when the curriculum consists of the most essential knowledge about ourselves and our world and when we focus on teaching skills for lifelong learning and working. For, if the real purpose of education is to create citizens who can live in and contribute to a democratic society, then we must include all of our students in our classrooms and teach them "what matters most." When we do this, all students, including those who have a disability, can be successful learners and members of our school communities.

Quick-Guides to Inclusion 3: Ideas for Educating Students with Disabilities © Michael F. Giangreco 2002
Available through Paul H. Brookes Publishing Co., Baltimore: 1-800-638-3775

#2

Teach Students to Care About Learning by Caring About Them

Teach Students to Care About Learning by Caring About Them

What was it about school that made you want to become a teacher? Did you love your subject matter so much that you just had to share it with others? Did a specific teacher in your educational career really ignite your passion for learning because she cared about you as an individual? It was probably a combination of both.

Students in high school—all students—need teachers who care about them and about their learning. Believing that all students can and *do* learn is a core value that teachers in an inclusive high school share. They believe strongly in giving every student the benefit of the doubt regarding their competence and "intelligence," even students who may have great difficulty showing what they know and understand because they don't have an effective communication system. After all, we know that our own caring, passion for learning, and expectations for success influence student performance!

The old adage, "They don't care how much you know until they know how much you care" characterizes high school learners. Adolescents respond best to teachers who know their names, treat them with respect in the classroom, create a classroom climate that is free of humiliation, grade fairly, follow through with promises, and respect their privacy. Once students know that their teachers care, they are ready to learn the course content from teachers who are as passionate about their subject area as they are about their students' learning. These great teachers present information in ways that respect the individual differences that students bring to the classroom, believing that knowledge, literacy, and the commitment to lifelong learning are important for each and every one.

Quick-Guides to Inclusion 3: Ideas for Educating Students with Disabilities © Michael F. Giangreco 2002
Available through Paul H. Brookes Publishing Co., Baltimore: 1-800-638-3775

#3

Figure Out How Every Student Is "Smart"

Figure Out How Every Student Is "Smart"

Imagine that you are attending a teacher's conference, and when you walk into the lecture hall, there are no tables and no chairs. Although the speaker's presentation is enlightening and humorous, after 15 minutes you notice that everyone in the room is starting to get a little "antsy." They begin to shift from foot to foot, and their attention wanders. One by one, people start to talk among themselves—some even leave the hall. Then, you see a colleague who appears calm and comfortable, sitting in her wheelchair, taking notes. Who has the disability in this situation? It is often said that including students with disabilities requires that we look "beyond" their labels. We contend that we need to do something even more radical—we need to change our whole notion of what disability is and develop a new way of looking at human differences. Just as the notion of disability takes on a new meaning in the previous example, so does the concept of *intelligence* if we think about the situations in which students perform well or poorly.

We all know students who are great writers but are unable to carry a tune; students who can fix a car but can't write a coherent paragraph; and students who can solve complicated math problems but have little insight into their own emotions or the feelings of others. How "smart" people seem depends on how they are asked to show their smartness and what society values. And, although society has a place for people of varied talents, schools focus almost exclusively on one or two areas. Our challenge as teachers is to find out how every one of our students is smart, to teach using methods that tap into different intelligences, and to stretch all of our students to develop their talents in all areas. If we do this, differences become ordinary, and no student seems out of place in our classroom.

Quick-Guides to Inclusion 3: Ideas for Educating Students with Disabilities © Michael F. Giangreco 2002
Available through Paul H. Brookes Publishing Co., Baltimore: 1-800-638-3775

#4

Make Learning Relevant Through the Study of "Essential Questions"

Make Learning Relevant Through the Study of "Essential Questions"

When high school classrooms are comprised of students of varying interests, talents, experiences, learning styles, and motivations, following a traditional, lecture-based approach to teaching just won't work. This is particularly true if what we want all students to know and be able to do goes beyond rote memorization and recall of a set of disconnected names, places, dates, and events. Designing units of study around an underlying *essential question* or in response to a real-life problem allows students to answer the question or solve the problem in unique ways that tap into their talents and bypass their academic challenges.

"What is worth fighting for?" is an essential question that might organize a semester's work in American history from the Revolutionary War through Reconstruction. "If we can, should we?" might be the central question for a biology unit on genetics and heredity. Posing these questions on the first day of class would undoubtedly engage each and every student in a lively discussion that is based mostly on personal opinion and experience. As the teacher introduces and elaborates the content of the unit, she helps students make connections between the lessons of history and science and their own lives.

Other content areas lend themselves to the use of *problem-based learning* in which teachers engage students in studying and solving real-life problems such as, "Design a child's toy that runs on solar power" or "Design a business plan for a student-run school store." The skills that are taught are those that students will need in order to solve the problem, providing a focus for instruction that goes beyond basic acquisition of knowledge to practical application and synthesis.

Quick-Guides to Inclusion 3: Ideas for Educating Students with Disabilities © Michael F. Giangreco 2002
Available through Paul H. Brookes Publishing Co., Baltimore: 1–800–638–3775

#5

Make
Learning Cooperative

Make Learning Cooperative

Do you remember teachers in high school who encouraged their students to work together on homework, labs, or projects? Their classrooms were a hotbed of activity and conversation, and you could just feel the excitement when students were encouraged to bounce ideas off one another.

Group activities are one of the ways in which teachers ensure that learning is active and interactive. Effective grouping meets individual student needs because activities are planned that value and build on differences in what students know, precisely because every student brings something unique to the group.

Instead of tracking and ability grouping, teachers in inclusive high schools use cooperative groups and peer supports to capitalize on student differences. In well-designed cooperative group activities, each student has a specific role and several tasks to accomplish for the group. Cooperative group assignments are designed so that every member of the group must do his or her part to accomplish the activity. For example, in a social studies class, groups of students may adopt a country and attempt to defend this country during a simulation of the events in World War II. Each group would need researchers, speechwriters, chart makers, speakers, and liaisons to other countries.

Peer supports can also be used in high school classes to ensure that students with disabilities participate in meaningful ways in the curriculum. For example, a peer may provide a voice for a student who does not speak, take notes for a student who has difficulty writing, or redirect a student with attention difficulties. When all students learn together, each student learns more.

#6

Allow Students a Variety of Ways to "Show What They Know"

Allow Students a Variety of Ways to "Show What They Know"

All of us have known students who performed terribly on "the test," yet we were certain that they understood the material. We remember saying, "Nathan, I can't understand why you didn't do better on this examination. I know you know this stuff. What happened?"

For many students, including those with disabilities, traditional ways of evaluating learning—pop quizzes, multiple choice questions, essay tests—don't reflect what's important about what we taught nor do they measure reliably what our students learned. In the inclusive high school classroom, effective teachers evaluate students as they are learning, rather than simply for the purpose of grading. They structure performance-based evaluations and final "exhibitions" that require students to demonstrate higher level skills such as judgment, application, and synthesis. This lets students use their most comfortable "intelligence" when learning new or personally challenging material. This requires students to stretch beyond their preferred mode of expression when working in collaborative groups or with supportive help from the teacher.

For example, a science teacher might give students many choices for how they demonstrate their evolving understanding of molecular bonding, such as explaining the concept in writing, using chemical symbols to show electron exchange, drawing diagrams or building models of compounds, or orchestrating a dance that shows how elements regroup to form new compounds. A history teacher could let students who love nature explore the influences of local topography and harsh weather on the outcome of various Civil War battles (Armstrong, 2000, p. 94). All students do their best work when they have both choice and challenge.

Quick-Guides to Inclusion 3: Ideas for Educating Students with Disabilities © Michael F. Giangreco 2002
Available through Paul H. Brookes Publishing Co., Baltimore: 1-800-638-3775

#7

When Students
Need Intensive
Supports, Provide Them
as Naturally as Possible

Quick-Guides to Inclusion 3: Ideas for Educating Students with Disabilities © Michael F. Giangreco 2002
Available through Paul H. Brookes Publishing Co., Baltimore: 1-800-638-3775

When Students Need Intensive Supports, Provide Them as Naturally as Possible

The provision of supports in a thoughtful way can make the difference between a student merely being "in" an inclusive environment—just physically present—and truly being "with" the other students—communicating, learning, and establishing social relationships.

When planning lessons to actively involve all students, the first question we should ask is, "Can this student participate in this activity just like all the other students?" Many times the answer is "yes," and no extra supports are needed. When students do need supports in order to fully participate, they tend to cluster in five interrelated categories.

1. *Physical, emotional, and sensory supports* might include assisting a student to move from his wheelchair to a stationary bicycle in gym class or giving a calming touch while he types out a message on an augmentative communication device.

2. A teacher might *modify the materials and/or provide technology* by converting test items that require written responses into multiple choice questions that can be programmed into a student's augmentative communication device.

3. *Personalized instruction* can be as simple as reinforcing directions or asking each student in the class a slightly different question during group discussions.

4. Allowing a student to build a model of a cell instead of writing a lab report can assess the same knowledge but *personalizes the demonstration of learning.*

5. As long as our grading systems are not designed to reflect the diversity of learners in our schools, some students may need *individualized grading plans* that represent their progress and achievement on individualized learning priorities that are addressed within inclusive activities and environments.

Quick-Guides to Inclusion 3: Ideas for Educating Students with Disabilities © Michael F. Giangreco 2002
Available through Paul H. Brookes Publishing Co., Baltimore: 1-800-638-3775

#8

Embed Social Justice Values in the Curriculum and Your Classroom

---

Embed Social Justice Values in the Curriculum and Your Classroom

Preparation for college and the world of work are important goals of a high school education. However, it is also essential that we prepare our students to be contributing citizens in a democracy. One of the responsibilities of our citizenship is the ability to live peacefully with others who are different from ourselves and to fight injustice whenever we see it—in other words, to work for social justice.

To facilitate students' commitment to this cause, teachers can address social justice issues through the curriculum and through their personal actions. Rather than stopping the flow of a course to have "disability awareness week," teachers can identify natural opportunities to discuss these issues. While reading *Of Mice and Men* (Steinbeck, 1937), an English teacher might highlight the need for everyone to have friends and advocates. Social studies students might study the World War II T4 killing program in which children with disabilities were the focus of Nazi experiments. In a child development course, the teacher might explore why people offer sympathy rather than congratulations when they hear that a friend has given birth to a child with a disability. In science, the teacher may discuss seizures during a lab on the central nervous system.

Establishing norms for how students and teachers treat one another extends the commitment to social justice beyond the curriculum to everyday interactions. Banning the use of hate speech and teaching students to mediate disagreements are part of the "hidden" yet essential curriculum in inclusive schools. Teachers in inclusive high schools show students that striving for social justice is in their best interest because there comes a time in everyone's life when we need others to stand up alongside and for us.

Quick-Guides to Inclusion 3: Ideas for Educating Students with Disabilities © Michael F. Giangreco 2002
Available through Paul H. Brookes Publishing Co., Baltimore: 1-800-638-3775

#9

Become a Reflective Practitioner with Other Teachers in Your School

---

Become a Reflective Practitioner with Other Teachers in Your School

Taking on a new challenge, such as including students with disabilities, tests many of the assumptions we all hold about teaching and learning. And like any other innovation, sustaining new practices and ways of thinking is probably harder than taking the first few steps. How do we avoid a return to the "status quo" or teacher burnout when there are more questions than answers? From our experience with inclusive high schools all around the country, teachers who engage in ongoing "reflective practice" seem to be able to keep up their enthusiasm, to work through tough problems, and to keep learning more about what works well. Taking reflection beyond the end-of-the-day thinking that we do on the drive home from school, however, means moving beyond our personal musings to making changes in our teaching that improve student learning. Because many minds are better than one, this is best accomplished by being a member of a small group of teachers who meet together regularly in "reflective practice groups."

Finding time together can be difficult, to say the least, but many high schools are restructuring their schedules to give teachers a common planning period during the school day to do this important work. With the helpful guidance of a facilitator, teachers can ask their colleagues to help them brainstorm ideas for inclusive teaching while they are planning a unit. They can work in pairs to observe in one another's classrooms, asking, "Is each and every student an active participant in both the academic and social life of this learning community?" They can reflect on "critical incidents" in their day-to-day teaching. And perhaps most importantly, they can examine student work as an indicator of how effectively instruction and supports are designed and implemented.

Quick-Guides to Inclusion 3: Ideas for Educating Students with Disabilities © Michael F. Giangreco 2002
Available through Paul H. Brookes Publishing Co., Baltimore: 1–800–638–3775

#10

Advocate
for Untracking
and the Inclusion
of All Students

Advocate for Untracking and the Inclusion of All Students

As a teacher, you have a tremendous amount of control over what goes on in your classroom. Although you probably need to address state or district standards and curriculum frameworks, it is generally your responsibility to decide how to design your room, the content of daily lessons, and to exercise your own unique instructional style. You may wonder, however, if your inclusive classroom practices are affected by—and can affect—the rest of the school. You see the benefits of having students with disabilities in your classroom, but you wonder why there are still separate special education classes, low- and high-level tracks, and alternative high schools. You don't know if it is really your business to address these inequities.

In our experience, unless all teachers do take on the role of "teacher as leader" in their schools, they will find that their own classroom practice is negatively affected by outdated philosophies, too little classroom support for students with learning challenges, and a lack of quality professional development.

All around the country, teachers are becoming involved in efforts to untrack schools and include all students. They are asking how race, economics, gender, and disability affect the inclusion or segregation of students. They are questioning the effectiveness of special education classes and asking that supports and services follow students into general education classes. Teachers like you—who may have started by making a difference in the life of just one student—are recognizing Margaret Mead's wisdom that "…a small group of committed citizens can change the world. Indeed it is the only thing that ever has" (as cited in Warner, 1992).

Selected References

Armstrong, T. (2000). *Multiple intelligences in the classroom (2nd ed.).* Alexandria, VA: Association for Supervision and Curriculum Development.

Delisle, R. (1997). *How to use problem-based learning in the classroom.* Alexandria, VA: Association for Supervision and Curriculum Development.

Fried, R. (1995). *The passionate teacher.* Boston: Beacon Press.

Gardner, H. (1983). *Frames of mind: The theory of multiple intelligences.* New York: Basic Books.

Jorgensen, C. (1998). *Restructuring high schools for all students: Taking inclusion to the next level.* Baltimore: Paul H. Brookes Publishing Co.

Sizer, T. (1984). *Horace's compromise.* Boston: Houghton Mifflin.

Steinbeck, J. (1937). *Of mice and men.* New York: Modern Library.

Tomlinson, C.A. (1999). *The differentiated classroom: Responding to the needs of all learners.* Alexandria, VA: Association for Supervision and Curriculum Development.

Warner, C. (1992). *The last word: A treasury of women's quotes.* Upper Saddle River, NJ: Prentice-Hall.

Assisting Students Who Use Wheelchairs: Guidelines for School Personnel

Michael F. Giangreco, Irene McEwen,
Timothy Fox, and Deborah Lisi-Baker

Quick-Guides to Inclusion 3:
Ideas for Educating Students with Disabilities

Michael F. Giangreco
Series Editor

ASSISTING STUDENTS WHO USE WHEELCHAIRS

Some students who use wheelchairs are quite capable of getting around using their own power or a motorized chair. Even when students are adept at using their wheelchairs, they will occasionally find themselves in situations where they need assistance. Some students may need more help, such as with transferring in and out of their wheelchairs or moving from place to place.

If you see a student struggling to overcome a barrier, such as trying to open a heavy door to enter a room, don't automatically assume that he needs or wants your help. Your best bet is to do the same thing you would do if you saw any student you thought could use some help. First, ask the student if he wants your assistance. If the answer is "Yes," then you can ask, "What kind of help would you like?" Most students who need this kind of occasional assistance can effectively communicate the assistance they need and exactly what they would find helpful.

Students who have limited language skills, lack a formal language system, or rely primarily on nonsymbolic forms of communication (e.g., facial expressions, vocalizations, pointing) may have difficulty communicating, especially with people who don't know them well. In these cases, if you really want to help, then you have to be willing to look and listen. A student who has been in her wheelchair for too long without a break, for example, may make certain sounds or move in ways that suggest she is uncomfortable. You have to interpret those nonsymbolic communications as best you can. You might guess her message is, "I want to get out of this chair!" If the student sighs with relief when she gets out of her chair, then you can feel reasonably sure you interpreted her communication correctly. Over time and with information provided by people who know the student well, you can become increasingly skillful in interpreting a student's nonsymbolic communication. You can also create language boards or use computer programs to make it easier for a student to let you know her needs.

Quick-Guides to Inclusion 3: Ideas for Educating Students with Disabilities © Michael F. Giangreco 2002
Available through Paul H. Brookes Publishing Co., Baltimore: 1-800-638-3775

Transferring to and from a Wheelchair

The following sections offer suggestions for assisting students with transferring to and from a wheelchair and with wheelchair mobility.

Students who use wheelchairs rarely sit in them all day long. Students need to transfer to and from a toilet, the floor, other equipment, or furniture. These position changes are important to prevent fatigue, discomfort, skin breakdown, and muscle tightness, which can occur when students sit in one position for too long.

Changes in position are not always for physical or health reasons. Changing positions can also be important to allow students with disabilities to participate in classroom activities. If the class moves from an activity where everyone is seated at desks to one where they are on the floor, for example, then the student who uses a wheelchair should be supported to join his classmates on the floor. The student may need a little or a lot of support to be comfortable and stable while he is out of his wheelchair. Supports can be as sophisticated as a specialized floor-sitting device or as simple as a wall to lean against, a pillow, or a friend to sit next to. As a general rule of thumb, the supports provided should meet the student's need in a manner that allows him to participate in the activity and fit in with the group. In other words, use the most typical support that works before using something unnecessarily specialized.

A student's physical therapist or occupational therapist can recommend general guidelines for how often a student should change positions. Of course, therapists are not around all of the time, so it is most important to listen to the student and encourage him to communicate his needs to change positions.

Quick-Guides to Inclusion 3: Ideas for Educating Students with Disabilities © Michael F. Giangreco 2002
Available through Paul H. Brookes Publishing Co., Baltimore: 1-800-638-3775

To help a student move to and from her wheelchair, you must learn how to make those transfers safely and comfortably for the student and for yourself. Before attempting to transfer a student, be sure to learn how to help this particular student from someone who knows the student well. That person might be the student herself, her parent, a teacher, a physical therapist, or an occupational therapist.

Most students can assist with one or more steps involved in a wheelchair transfer. Always expect students to assist as much as possible with every step of a transfer. Be sure to give students enough time to do what they are capable of doing. Specific steps in the transfer will vary depending on where the student is transferring. An assisted transfer to the floor, for example, will be different than a transfer to a couch.

Young children, because of their size, tend to be easier to transfer. Because young children are easy to lift, the tendency is to do too much for the student. If young students are not allowed to learn and practice the skills they need to use in transferring, then as they grow older and heavier, the task of transferring becomes more difficult. Every opportunity to practice transferring is an important opportunity for learning. With each transfer, the student can be practicing communication, social, and movement skills involved in the transfer. Learning to transfer independently, or with as little assistance as possible, can allow students more independence in their daily lives and can open opportunities that may otherwise be limited.

Because of the inherent risks in transferring students to and from their wheelchairs, both to the student with a disability and the people providing assistance, it is always advisable to err on the side of caution. For example, trying to transfer a student by yourself, when a two-person transfer makes more sense, can result in either the student or you being injured. A physical therapist can show you how to maintain your body position to minimize your own risk of back injury.

Quick-Guides to Inclusion 3: Ideas for Educating Students with Disabilities © Michael F. Giangreco 2002
Available through Paul H. Brookes Publishing Co., Baltimore: 1–800–638–3775

Transferring from a Wheelchair

The following steps offer a general sequence for transferring *from* a wheelchair. The specific steps can vary greatly from student to student, and the order may vary slightly.

1. Let the student know that it is time to transfer.
2. Always minimize the distance between transfer points. If the student is able, ask him to move his wheelchair to the proper position for the transfer. If not, inform the student of your intention, and move the chair into position yourself.
3. Once in position, have the student lock the brakes on the wheelchair. If necessary, lock the brakes yourself.
4. Remove equipment and supports that may get in the way. For example,
   - Remove the lap tray and any switches or other devices.
   - Loosen the footstraps and move the footrests to the side.
   - Remove the block (e.g., abductor block) from between the knees.
   - Remove any chest, shoulder, or head straps.
   - Remove or adjust one side support (e.g., arm rest) in some cases.
5. Ask the student to lean forward.
6. Unfasten the seat belt.
7. While still leaning forward from the trunk and hips, ask the student to slide forward in the chair and put his feet on the floor.
8. Ask the student to stand up—this may require your assistance. Most students, regardless of the severity of the disability, can bear some weight, particularly if the student has been expected to bear weight since a young age. The ability to support at least partial weight during standing is extremely important, and students need to practice whenever they transfer. Except in emergencies (which are rare), never lift a

Quick-Guides to Inclusion 3: Ideas for Educating Students with Disabilities © Michael F. Giangreco 2002
Available through Paul H. Brookes Publishing Co., Baltimore: 1–800–638–3775

student who can support any of his own weight. For your own health and safety while assisting the student, be sure to maintain good body alignment (i.e., straight back, bending from the knees).

9. Assist the student to move to the other surface as you have been shown by a knowledgeable person (e.g., therapist, parent). Make sure the student is comfortably and safely positioned before moving away.

10. Release the brakes on the wheelchair, and move it to an appropriate location until it is needed again.

Quick-Guides to Inclusion 3: Ideas for Educating Students with Disabilities © Michael F. Giangreco 2002
Available through Paul H. Brookes Publishing Co., Baltimore: 1-800-638-3775

Transferring to a Wheelchair

The following steps offer a general sequence for transferring to a wheelchair. The specific steps can vary greatly from student to student, and the order may vary slightly.

1. Let the student know that it is time to transfer.
2. Always minimize the distance between transfer points.
3. Make sure the brakes of the wheelchair are locked.
4. Make sure the wheelchair is free of any supportive equipment that might get in the way of a successful transfer (e.g., footrests, blocks and straps, seat belt).
5. Assist the student in assuming a standing position next to the wheelchair, as you have been shown by a knowledgeable person (e.g., therapist, parent). Maintain a proper body position to minimize your own risk of back injury.
6. Assist the student to turn and sit on the edge of the seat.
7. Ask the student to lean forward, and, if necessary, assist the student to get situated as far back into the chair as possible.
8. While the student is still leaning forward, make sure the student is all the way back in the chair and is centered (i.e., not closer to one side of the chair than the other); this is extremely important. If the student is not centered and situated all the way back in the wheelchair, then the student's posture will be poor. This will lead to discomfort and fatigue.
9. While the student is still leaning forward, *fasten the seat belt*. Just like in a car or airplane, the belt should be secured snug and low across the lap to keep the student positioned properly. This is especially important for students who have difficulty repositioning themselves in their wheelchairs. Students who are able to reposition themselves will make their own adjustments to the seat belt's tension.

10. Attach or fasten equipment and adjust the student's positioning supports. For example,
    - Adjust the footrests and position the student's feet.
    - Place and secure any blocks or supports (e.g., abductor block).
    - Attach and secure any chest, shoulder, and head supports.
    - Attach the lap tray and any switches or other devices.
11. Ask the student to release the brakes, and you are ready to go.

Quick-Guides to Inclusion 3: Ideas for Educating Students with Disabilities © Michael F. Giangreco 2002
Available through Paul H. Brookes Publishing Co., Baltimore: 1–800–638–3775

Wheelchair Mobility

Many students can move their wheelchairs most of the time but may need help in some situations. Others need help most of the time, and some students need help all of the time. Regardless of how much help a student needs, always make sure students who are using their wheelchairs are wearing their seat belts and any other supports they might need to be comfortable and safe. Try to keep the following guidelines and ideas in mind.

Pushing a student's wheelchair without permission is like rudely shoving a student who can walk. Always ask permission to move students in their wheelchairs. If you see a student you think needs assistance, then you might ask, "Can I help you back up?" If a student can't move her own wheelchair, then let her know that you are going to move her—"It's time to go to lunch now, are you ready?" Pause to allow the student a moment to get ready to go. Then before moving her wheelchair, let her know your intentions by saying something such as, "Here we go!"

Turning off a student's power wheelchair to prevent the student from moving about is inappropriate. It is like tying a student who walks in a stationary chair. If the student is using his mobility in a way that is perceived as a problem, then address the behavior as you would a similar situation with a student who can walk. Consider the intention of the student's behavior. For example, is he trying to tell you he is bored, wants to escape the situation, or is more interested in something else he sees across the room? Once you have figured this out, do something constructive to address the identified issue.

Remember that a manual wheelchair is a mobility device—it is not an exercise device. If moving their wheelchairs is difficult for students, then they should not be expected to push themselves simply for exercise or so they won't get "lazy." Students who use

Quick-Guides to Inclusion 3: Ideas for Educating Students with Disabilities © Michael F. Giangreco 2002
Available through Paul H. Brookes Publishing Co., Baltimore: 1-800-638-3775

wheelchairs should be able to get around as easily as their classmates who walk and run. A power wheelchair may be necessary. If a student with a manual wheelchair needs help to keep up with friends, then try to teach a responsible friend to help, rather than having an adult help all the time. Clear this approach with the student and family, and make sure the student-helper is oriented to safe and respectful ways to offer assistance to people who use wheelchairs.

Talk with students when you push their wheelchairs, just as you would if you were walking with a student who does not use a wheelchair. In some situations, where the space is wide, flat, and smooth enough (e.g., wide hallways), you can actually push a student's wheelchair while walking beside, rather than behind, her. This is not possible in all situations. It is most likely to be an option when the person providing assistance is quite a bit larger than the person in the wheelchair thus allowing the person to adequately control the wheelchair with one hand. Use your judgment and only walk beside while pushing the person's wheelchair in situations where it normally is courteous to walk side by side. This would not be a good idea when the halls are crowded between classes at a high school, for example, but would be if the student using a wheelchair and a peer are running an errand while the halls are empty.

Quick-Guides to Inclusion 3: Ideas for Educating Students with Disabilities © Michael F. Giangreco 2002
Available through Paul H. Brookes Publishing Co., Baltimore: 1-800-638-3775

Other Mobility Tips

1. Push students in wheelchairs forward up ramps. Go down steep or long ramps backward, particularly if the student is not able to lean back. Imagine what might happen if you lost your grip on a student's wheelchair and he headed down a long ramp, unable to stop himself—it's not a pleasant thought!

2. To help a student *go up a curb* (if no curb cut exists), first move the student in the wheelchair forward until the front (small) wheels are near the curb. Let the student know you plan to tip the chair back slightly to get up the curb. Then tip the wheelchair onto its back wheels by pushing down on the push handles while stepping down on one of the tip bars (near the ground, inside the wheels) with your foot. Push the chair forward and put the front wheels on the sidewalk (some students can push on the hand rims or power their chair to help). When the back wheels almost reach the curb, lift the chair by the push handles, and roll the back wheels up onto the sidewalk (some students also can help during this step).

3. To help a student *go down a curb* (if no curb cut exists), first move the student in the wheelchair backward until the back wheels (the large ones) are near the edge of the curb. Let the student know you plan to tip the chair back slightly to get down the curb. Then move the wheelchair back by holding onto the push handles and supporting the wheelchair while rolling the back wheels down the curb (some students can help by holding the hand rim to slow the descent). Roll the wheelchair back until the front wheels are near the edge of the curb. Still holding onto the push handles, slowly roll the front wheels down the curb. Turn around, and you are on your way.

4. When curbs, stairs, or other barriers exist, consider joining together with people who have disabilities to advocate for changes (e.g., curb cuts, ramps, elevators) that allow uni-

Quick-Guides to Inclusion 3: Ideas for Educating Students with Disabilities © Michael F. Giangreco 2002
Available through Paul H. Brookes Publishing Co., Baltimore: 1-800-638-3775

versal access. Although you may have been prompted to think about these barriers because of a student you know who uses a wheelchair, these types of changes can allow better or easier access for many other people (e.g., a parent with an infant in a stroller, a delivery person with a heavy load, a person who is temporarily on crutches, an elderly person who has difficulty with stairs).

5. Be aware that some students, particularly those with difficulty controlling their trunk and head, may need extra supports (e.g., head strap) when traveling in the school bus or being moved over uneven surfaces, such as when participating in field sports during recess or physical education class.

6. When assisting students in their wheelchairs on the playground or ball fields, it is often advisable to tip the wheelchair slightly onto the large rear wheels. As in all cases, always let the student know what you plan to do before doing it. When running the bases in a softball game or running on a field while playing ultimate frisbee, for example, the small wheels of a wheelchair often get caught in the ruts and uneven surfaces. This can cause the wheelchair to tip forward unexpectedly. This is a prime situation where having the seat belt fastened is critical—without it, the student can easily be thrown from the wheelchair. So let the student experience the faster than normal speed of running the bases and playing in the field by tipping the chair on its rear wheels and maintaining a safe speed.

Make sure every member of the school team, including the student and the student's parents, is aware of these general guidelines. More importantly, make sure those providing assistance understand the individual needs and preferences of the student. It is helpful to document a student's mobility needs and preferences in writing or with photos to orient school personnel, classmates, and friends in the safe and respectful ways to offer assistance.

Quick-Guides to Inclusion 3: Ideas for Educating Students with Disabilities © Michael F. Giangreco 2002
Available through Paul H. Brookes Publishing Co., Baltimore: 1-800-638-3775

Get more user-friendly advice on inclusion with
Quick-Guides 1 & 2!

Set up just like *Quick-Guides 3*, these effective guides will help
you make inclusion work in any school—on any budget!

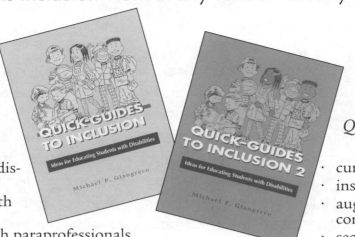

Quick-Guides to Inclusion
gives you suggestions for

· including students with disabilities in the classroom
· building partnerships with
  parents
· creating partnerships with paraprofessionals
· getting the most out of support services
· creating positive behavioral supports

Stock Number: 3033   Price: $22.95
1997 · 160 pages · 8 ¹/₂ x 11
spiral-bound · ISBN 1-55766-303-3

Quick-Guides to Inclusion 2
provides information on

· curriculum adaptations
· instructional strategies
· augmentative and alternative
  communication
· secondary transition
· administration of inclusive
  schools

Stock Number: 3351   Price: $22.95
1998 · 160 pages · 8 ¹/₂ x 11
spiral-bound · ISBN 1-55766-335-1

PLACE YOUR ORDER NOW! ‒ ‒ ‒ ‒ ‒ ‒ ‒ ‒ ‒ ‒ ‒ ‒ ‒ ‒ ‒ ‒ ‒

Please send me

___ **Quick Guides to Inclusion** / Stock #3033 / $22.95
___ **Quick Guides to Inclusion 2** / Stock #3351 / $22.95

___ Check enclosed (payable to Brookes Publishing Co.)
___ Purchase Order attached (bill my institution)
___ Please charge my credit card: ○ American Express   ○ MasterCard   ○ Visa

Photocopy this form and mail it to
Brookes Publishing Co., P.O. Box 10624,
Baltimore, MD 21285-0624; FAX **410-337-8539;**
call toll-free (8 A.M. – 5 P.M. ET)
1-800-638-3775 or **410-337-9580**
(outside the U.S.); or order online at
www.brookespublishing.com

Credit Card #: _____   Exp. Date: _____

Signature (required with credit card use): _____

Name: _____ Daytime phone: _____

Street Address: _____   ❑ residential ❑ commercial
Orders cannot be shipped to P.O. boxes

City/State/ZIP: _____   Country: _____

E-mail Address: _____
❑ Yes! I want to receive special web site discount offers! My e-mail address will not be shared with any other party.

Product Total $_____

FOR ORDERS WITHIN THE CONTINENTAL U.S.
Shipping Rates for UPS Ground delivery*
If your product total (before tax) is:
$0.00 to $49.99, add $5.00
$50.00 to $399.99, add 10% of product total
$400.00 and over, add 8% of product total
*For rush orders call **1-800-638-3775**.
For international orders call **410-337-9580**.

Policies and prices subject to change without
notice. Prices may be higher outside the U.S.

You may return books within 30 days for a
full credit of the product price. Refunds will
be issued for prepaid orders. Items must be
returned in resalable condition.

Shipping Rate (see chart) $_____
Maryland Orders add 5%
sales tax (to product total only) $_____

Grand Total U.S. $_____
Your source code is **BA 64**

Browse our entire catalog, read excerpts, and find special offers at *www.brookespublishing.com*